Season of Repentance

Season of Repentance

Lenten Homilies
of Saint John of Kronstadt

Saint John of Kronstadt
(Ivan Ilyich Sergiev)

Translated by
Sergio Tancredo Sette Câmara e Silva

Holy Trinity Publications
The Printshop of St Job of Pochaev
Holy Trinity Monastery
Jordanville, New York

Printed with the blessing of His Eminence,
Metropolitan Hilarion First Hierarch
of the Russian Orthodox Church Outside of Russia

Season of Repentance: Lenten Homilies of St John of Kronstadt
© 2015 Holy Trinity Monastery

HOLY TRINITY PUBLICATIONS
The Printshop of St Job of Pochaev
Holy Trinity Monastery
Jordanville, New York 13361-0036
www.holytrinitypublications.com

ISBN: 978-0-88465-384-4 (paperback)
ISBN: 978-0-88465-393-6 (ePub)
ISBN: 978-0-88465-394-3 (Mobipocket)

Library of Congress Control Number 2014955762

Cover Design: James Bozeman
Photo © 2014 Kelleylynn Rainville Barberg

Scripture passages taken from the New King James Version.
Copyright © 1982 by Thomas Nelson, Inc. Used by permission.
Deuterocanonical passages taken from the Orthodox Study Bible.
Copyright © 2008 by Thomas Nelson, Inc. Used by permission.
Psalms taken from *A Psalter for Prayer*, trans. David James
(Jordanville, N.Y.: Holy Trinity Publications, 2011).

CONTENTS

Saint John of Kronstadt
Oil on Canvas: Archimandrite Cyprian (Pyzhov)

INTRODUCTION

St John of Kronstadt (1829–1908) is the most renowned saint of the Orthodox Church in Russia in the half century leading up to the Bolshevik Revolution of 1917. He was born Ivan Ilyich Sergiev, in the small town of Sura near the White Sea coast of northern Russia. He received a vision during childhood and was called to service in the Church as a priest. In addition, he was miraculously healed of early learning disabilities. His life and preaching went on to touch millions, not only in Kronstadt, the Imperial Naval port by St Petersburg where his parish was found, but throughout the Russian Empire and even into the Western world.

The extent of the wider world's awareness of St John of Kronstadt is evidenced in the writings of Andrew Dickson White, the co-founder and first President of Cornell University in Ithaca, New York. In 1892 White became the American First Minister to Russia and referred to learning more about Father Ivan "as a matter of special interest." This extract from White's memoirs offers a vivid description of the future saint's life and ministry:

> There is at present on the island of Cronstadt [Kronstadt], at the mouth of the Neva, a Russo-Greek priest, Father Ivan [John], who enjoys throughout the empire a vast reputation as a saintly worker of miracles. This priest has a very spiritual and kindly face; is known to receive vast sums for the poor, which he distributes among them while he himself remains in poverty; and is supposed not merely by members of the Russo-Greek Church, but by those of other religious bodies, to work frequently miracles of healing. I was assured by persons of the highest character—and those not only Russo-Greek churchmen, but Roman Catholics and Anglicans—that there could be no doubt as to the reality of these miracles, and various examples were given to me. So great is Father Ivan's reputation in this respect that he is in constant demand in all parts of the empire, and was even summoned to Livadia [the summer home in the Crimea of the Russian imperial family] during the last illness of the late Emperor [Tsar Alexander III]. Whenever he appears in public, great crowds surround him seeking to touch the hem of his garment. His picture is to be seen with the portraits of the saints in vast numbers of Russian homes,

from the palaces of the highest nobles to the cottages of the humblest peasants.[1]

To twenty-first-century Christians, St John is probably best known through his spiritual journals, *My Life in Christ*, published by this monastery in English translation. We are now pleased to offer this selection of his Lenten sermons in English translation for the first time, which we hope will equally touch the lives of many.

---

[1] Andrew Dickson White, *Autobiography of Andrew D. White*, vol. II (New York: The Century Co., 1905).

On the Sunday of the Publican and the Pharisee

The Pharisee stood and prayed thus with himself, 'God, I thank You that I am not like other men—extortioners, unjust, adulterers, or even as this tax collector[publican].' (Luke 18:11)

Being teachers of the faith among the Jewish people, the Pharisees were praised for their knowledge of the Law and were, at the same time, the ones who dishonored God the most by transgressing the Law and by their extreme hypocrisy. The Saviour showed his understanding of them very well when He said that they love to take the highest seats at the synagogues and to be greeted in the market. This unfortunate passion of self-exaltation originated in them because of a false exaggeration of their own merits for, as public teachers of the faith, they knew well the Mosaic Law, which many Jews did not know. The tax collectors, according to their rank, very often resorted to illegal means of extortion. In the Gospel we see the amazing example of humility and self-sacrifice of Zacchaeus, who was a chief tax collector. When the Saviour came to his house, Zacchaeus, feeling a deep sense of repentance, told the Lord: *Look, Lord, I give half of my goods to the poor; and if I have taken anything from anyone by false accusation, I restore fourfold* (Luke 19:8).

Pharisees and tax collectors, not in name, but according to their deeds, exist even in our time. The passion of self-exaltation and self-praise to this day reigns among the children of fallen Adam. Heeding the call of our Mother, the Church, let us discuss how dangerous this passion is and what can move us toward humility. Where does the passion of self-exaltation and self-praise in us come from? It comes from the same source where all of our sins originate: from the first, ancestral sin. Man was created in order to love God, as He was the cause of man's being, and in order to contemplate God's perfection and to imitate Him, faithfully fulfilling His will. But man loved himself more than he loved God, and desired to usurp His perfection, to be as great as God, and to be his own master; thus, he subjected himself to self-love and pride, and he fell. Therefore, self-exaltation, or pride, is a passion that is spiritually fatal to man, which makes him hostile to God and contemptuous toward his neighbors. Can God look with favor toward a creature who puffs up his own perfections and finds no equal to them, as if we had something that is actually our own?

Here is the beginning of our passion of self-exaltation. As a passion, it is naturally one of our soul's infirmities, having infected our soul at the moment of the fall of the first people. As a false opinion regarding one's own perfection, as a movement of the will that goes against the law, this passion is also the fruit of the suggestions of that evil spirit, who himself fell due to pride and envy, and lured man to share his fall through these same sins. We know that our forefathers did not fall by themselves, but by the devil's temptation. Must we go on about how pride or self-praise, coupled with the humiliation of others, is a disease of our souls? In order to confirm this, one need simply to look upon a proud man with the eyes of holy faith. What is a man in his present state? He is fallen, broken, covered with wounds. Do you think this comparison is exaggerated? Recall the parable of the Good Samaritan and the man who fell among robbers (Luke 10:30–37). Who does the man who fell among robbers, was beaten and wounded, represent? Who if not ourselves, tortured by passions, the world, and the devil? What if that man began to claim that he was perfectly healthy and that he feels no pain, what would we say about him? Would we not say that he is extremely sick and close to death because his body is no longer sensitive, capable of detecting in it the presence of health?

This is by all means the same that we can say about the man who is proud.

Pride, moreover, is the fruit of the suggestions of the evil spirit. Is it difficult to be convinced of this? Pride is a false, exaggerated opinion of one's own perfections, real or imaginary, coupled with the humiliation of others. A false opinion,... but where do lies come from? God is the Truth. The Holy Scripture indicates to us one source, one father of lies: *You are of your father the devil, and the desires of your father you want to do. He was a murderer from the beginning, and does not stand in the truth, because there is no truth in him. When he speaks a lie, he speaks from his own resources, for he is a liar and the father of it* (John 8:44). He then whispers to man, who is busy working on himself, performing good deeds, that he is the most perfect creature, by whom everyone must be amazed, and that all others are despicable creatures who lead vain lives and do nothing else but sin. Judge for yourselves how false this is. Does that man, arrogant and proud, who is the most perfect creature in the world, really exist? And what about his neighbors, so boldly offended by him, are they really that awful? Maybe it happened that at the same time that they were judged by him, they repented, wept for their sins before *He who searches the minds and hearts* (Rev 2:23), the God of all, and received forgiveness.

Meanwhile, the simple fact that someone praises himself, be it in church before God, or before everyone else, is already suspicious. True perfection, true virtue, is modest: it likes to hide in secret and does not dare ascribe to itself its own perfection, much less humiliate others. You say that you are kind, compassionate to all, zealous toward the faith and the Holy Church, and that you weaken your flesh through fasting. So far so good. But who gave you the right to refer to yourself with the names of these honored virtues? Who declared you good, compassionate, zealous toward the Church and her holy ordinances? Was it God? Was it an angel? Or did you yourself weigh up your own virtues? How can we appraise our own actions? How are we capable of weighing them? What is the measure we use? Do we know well our own impure hearts, which always, or at least very often, play a large part in the performance of good deeds? When taking into account our own virtues, do we include self-love or other unseemly motives? How easy it is sometimes to hide from our own consciousness the unseemly motives that were in fact the true reason for our good deeds. The poison of sin has penetrated deeply into our souls, and, unbeknownst to us, it poisons almost all of our virtues. Is it not better to scrutinize oneself more often and more closely, and to notice our faults in the depths of our soul in order to correct them, rather than to display externally our virtues? Actually, why should we display them externally, or praise ourselves, when the most impartial Judge of them is in heaven, our Lord God, Who can *give to every man according to his ways* (Jer 17:10) and certainly knows how to weigh up our deeds. Let us allow Him to judge our virtues, and without exaltation, *work out your own salvation in fear and trembling* (Phil 2:12).

We must not exalt ourselves before others, but we should rather humble ourselves. And how many reasons to humble ourselves do each of us have! Man possesses nothing of his own; all that he has he received from God: his soul, his body, everything that he has, except for sin. Every good deed also comes from God. What can man boast of? *And what do you have that you did not receive? Now if you did indeed receive it, why do you boast as if you had not received it?* (1 Cor 4:7). If he boasts of his virtues, then he blasphemes, ascribing to himself that glory that belongs to God alone. Furthermore, every person is more or less in a weak spiritual state. At the very least, very many people find themselves in a state of sinful insensitivity. This sickly, false confidence they have in themselves is so unbearable, and yet they feel completely healthy and feel no need of a physician. What more motive then do we have to not think highly of our good deeds than the fact that they are, perhaps, a delusion of our soul?

Our heavenly and omniscient Judge took it upon Himself to weigh up our deeds and will reward each of them in due time. How necessary it is, then, to perform each of our good deeds in the eyes of God and to give Him, and to Him alone, to judge them, not daring to approach them with our own sinful judgments. However, we must recognize that whatever good deeds we have are very few, and that we have incomparably more bad deeds than good.

And this is a new and the strongest motive toward humility: I am a sinner, and God is just. How can we not keep in mind the judgment of God, which may be ready to be accomplished in us this very day, and not forget, perhaps, the most insignificant of good works, which in comparison to our many sins does not mean anything; because we sin every day without fail, we sin every hour in word and deed, with our thoughts and with our feelings. Give us, O Lord, to have constantly before our eyes how we are totally and completely dependent on You, to have constantly before our eyes our weaknesses, our sinfulness, in order to constantly humble ourselves before You and before our neighbors.

Brothers and sisters! Without a shadow of a doubt we must appreciate the example of humility of the publican presented to us in today's Gospel reading, as he represents all of us, repentant sinners; and we will easily recognize and love our image, described to us in the Holy Scriptures; we must appreciate it especially because we have seen how he was pardoned by God for his humility and, although he was a great sinner, because publicans in general were immersed in oppression and bribery, *this man went down to his house justified* (Luke 18:14). Let us try to emulate this example of humility. Certainly no one would say that he is not a sinner, and that he has no reason to lament his own sins as did the publican, beating himself on the chest and humbly asking for forgiveness: *God, be merciful to me a sinner* (Luke 18:13).

We are all sinners in need of God's mercy. If the blood of the Lamb of God, Who takes away the sin of the world, had not interceded for us, then each day and every hour the blows of heavenly justice would rattle us; and every day our sinful souls would have lived and died in misery, and would taste neither joy nor peace, for all eternity. But the Son of God intercedes for us, and because of His merits our sins do not cry out so loudly, seeking to be avenged. God forgives us our sins as long as we are ready ourselves to acknowledge them and to repent of them. Yes, God forgives us our sins. We must only lament them, beg with all our hearts for forgiveness from the Lord Jesus, and He, through the grace and compassion of His love for mankind, forgives through His servant all the sins that burden our conscience. Imitating the humility of the publican, let us eradicate in us by all means the boasting of the Pharisee.

With what unpleasant features is the Pharisee depicted, who delights himself in his own virtues.

I am such and such, he says, not like other people, or like this publican I thank Thee, he says, for this. You do a good thing by thanking the Lord for good deeds because they do not come from us, but from God; but why boast, why exalt yourself before the face of God Himself, as if He did not know the worth of the good deeds? Why despise your own brother? Are you not the same man, condemned and sinful, as the publican; have your virtues suddenly transformed you into a pure and sinless angel? Have you performed these good deeds through your own strength? How can you have suddenly forgotten about your weakness and see only perfection, and not think even a little about humility, which you so sorely need? Why do you think you are a wonderful, virtuous man? With all your virtues, why do you not think that you have only done that which was your duty and remain that unprofitable servant, according to the words of the Saviour: *So likewise you, when you have done all those things which you are commanded, say, 'We are unprofitable servants. We have done what was our duty to do'* (Luke 17:10).

Lord! Without You, we *can do nothing* (John 15:5). Give us the humility of the publican and expel from us every thought of Pharisaical pride. And may we always remember that we are all Yours, with everything that we possess and see around us, and that we have nothing, absolutely nothing, of which to boast. Amen.

On the Sunday of the Publican and the Pharisee

According to the Church, the present Sunday is called the Sunday of the Publican and the Pharisee. It is so named because today we read in the Gospel the Lord's parable about the Publican and the Pharisee. In the parable, through the examples of the publican and the Pharisee, the Lord instructs us with what disposition of soul we ought to pray in church, or anywhere else, for that matter. We listen to how each of them prayed, which one of them pleased God through his prayer, and which one didn't; and in what way one of them pleased God, and the other didn't, in order that we may also learn how to always pray in a God-pleasing way, without condemnation. Prayer is a great thing; through prayer man communicates with God, receives from Him various gifts of grace; through prayer man thanks Him as Benefactor for His constant mercies, and praises Him as the all-perfect Creator.

The Pharisee and the Publican prayed in the temple. *Two men went up to the temple to pray, one a Pharisee, and the other a tax collector* (Luke 18:10). The Pharisee prayed, *God, I thank You that I am not like other men—extortioners, unjust, adulterers, or even as this tax collector. I fast twice a week; I give tithes of all that I possess* (Luke 18:11–12). The Publican did not pray like that at all. He didn't say much, but he did grieve much over his sins; he did not raise his head over others, but, with his face to the ground, from a strong sense of grief he struck his chest and only said: *God, be merciful to me a sinner* (Luke 8:13). Everyone knows whose prayer was pleasing to God, and whose wasn't: the Publican went home from the temple more justified, though he was a sinner; and the Pharisee didn't, even though he fulfilled the precepts of the Law.

How was the Publican's prayer pleasing to God? It was so because he was humble and had a contrite heart during prayer; and the Holy Prophet and King David long ago said, *A broken and a contrite heart—These, O God, You will not despise* (Ps 51:17).

And why was the prayer of the Pharisee not pleasing to God? One needs some discernment in order to answer this correctly. *Woe to those who are wise in their own eyes. And prudent in their own sight!* (Isa 5:21), says God through the prophet. The Pharisee, in his blind self-conceit and pride, has forgotten who he is and Whom he addresses: the sinner imagined himself to be a righteous man; the sinner forgot that he speaks with the All-seeing and All-just God.

My God! What are our good deeds, which we sometimes dare to boast of before people and before Thy face? Every one of our good deeds is of little importance because they come from an impure heart, taking from it a large portion of impurity, for example, the impurity of lack of faith, unbelief, self-love, false pretenses, vanity, pride, impatience, irritability, and so on; also, any good deed is done by us with the help of God, so that, without the Lord, according to His word, we *can do nothing* (John 15:5). There is no doubt that each one of us has incomparably more sins than good deeds. How can I, during prayer, remember my few good deeds, all accomplished with the help of God, when I have incomparably more wicked deeds? No, it is better for me to shed tears of contrition for my sins, better *to pour my ardent prayer to the Lord, and to Him reveal my sorrow, because my soul is filled with evil and my life draws closer to hades* (Irmos tone 8, 6th ode). Regarding my good deeds, if I have any, I will be silent, or altogether forget about them before the face of the Lord, in order not to imagine myself a righteous person, deserving of a reward from Him because of my virtues.

I must remember the words of the Lord that I must say every time I perform a good deed: *when you have done all those things which you are commanded, say,*

'We are unprofitable servants. We have done what was our duty to do' (Luke 17:10). How can I list the sins of others, when I have so many of my own? No, I will not act this way; I will not fall into so much delusion and self-esteem and see within myself only good things, ignoring what is bad; otherwise I will be possessed by the passions of self-love and pride, and I will in fact see within myself only good things, as did the Pharisee, and will forget about things within me which are much worse. No, it is better for me to say to the Lord more often: *grant me to see mine own faults, and not to judge my brother* (prayer of St Ephrem the Syrian). Let us pray, brethren, in this frame of mind, and our prayer will be pleasing to God and will serve toward our salvation. In our prayers, be they in church or at home, we need to have, without fail, humility before God and before people. Should not the sinner humble himself? The Lord has mercy on the sinners and saves them. *I was brought low, and He saved me* (Ps 116:6), says David. God, have mercy on us, sinners. Amen.

HOMILY 3

On the Sunday of the Prodigal Son

I will arise and go to my Father. (Luke 15:18)

Brethren! The parable of the Prodigal Son should absorb all of our attention. In it, as in a mirror, we can see each of us. The Lord, Who knows our hearts, in only a few words and in the person of a single man, presented to us how the deceptive sweetness of sin removes us from the true sweetness of life according to God, and how our experience of the burdens of sin, for the body and soul, leads us, through the action of Divine grace, to turn back to God. Many people do in fact turn back to God and to a life of virtue. Let us examine this parable and discuss how necessary and how convenient it is for the sinner to turn to God.

A man had two sons. When they came of age, the younger said to his father: give me the portion of the estate that belongs to me. And so the father divided the estate. The eldest son did not take his share, but remained with the father, a sign that he loved his father with a pure heart, and found satisfaction in fulfilling his will. *I never transgressed your commandment at any time* (Luke 15:29). He considered his brother, who left his father, to be mad. The younger son, a few days afterward, having gathered all that he owned, left his father's house and went far away, and there he lost all his possessions through dissolute living. From this we can see that he possessed neither a good nor a clean heart, that he was not sincerely disposed toward his good father, that being under his father's watch was a burden to him, and that he preferred to live according to the will of his depraved heart. But listen to what happened to him after he left his father's house. When he had dissolutely spent everything he had in a foreign country, there arose a mighty famine in those lands, and he began to live in want. And he went and joined himself to one of the citizens of that country, and this man sent him to his fields to tend to his swine. And he would have been happy to fill his belly with the feed (acorns and chaff) on which the swine fed; but no one would give it to him. Coming to his senses, he said: how many hired servants of my father have bread enough and to spare, and here I perish with hunger. I will arise and go to my father, and I will tell him: *Father! I have sinned against heaven and in your sight, and am no longer worthy to be called your son* (Luke 15:21). He arose and went to his father, and when he was still far away, his father saw him and took pity on him, and went out to meet him, embraced him and kissed him; he forgave him and took him into his home, dressed him in the best garments and made a feast on the occasion of his return. Thus the fallen son went back to the love of his father.

Brethren! Likewise does our Heavenly Father act toward us. He does not keep us with Him by force if we, having a dissolute and ungrateful heart, do not want to live according to His commandments; He allows us to go away from Him and to see by experience just how dangerous it is to live according to our own heart, what a painful feeling, lack of peace and tranquility the soul feels when it gives itself over to the passions, what shameful food it feeds on; for what can be more shameful than the food of our passions? But God forbid that anyone remain forever away from God; to be away from God, that is true and eternal perdition. *For indeed, those who are far from You shall perish* (Ps 73:27), says the Holy Prophet and King David. We must constantly turn from the disastrous path of sin back to God with all our heart; and let everyone be confident that the Lord sees his sincere repentance, goes out to meet him with love, and just as before counts him as one of His children.

Have you sinned? Say with full determination in your heart: *I will arise and go to my father* (Luke 15:18), and do go to Him. And as soon as you say these words in your heart, as soon as you decide firmly to live according to His will, He will immediately see that you come back to Him; He is always *not far from each one of us* (Acts 17:27), He will immediately pour in your heart His peace, you will suddenly have such a light and pleasant feeling, like, for example, an insolvent debtor feels when his debts are forgiven, or like a poor person feels when suddenly he is dressed in the best garments, or is made to sit at a rich table.

But at the same time, brethren, notice that there are just as many ways to return to the Heavenly Father as there are passions and sins: each sin or passion is a road that leads to a land that is away from God. Have you taken the road of disbelief? Come back, be aware of its folly, feel with all your heart its heaviness, emptiness, perdition, and set firm foot on the path of faith, which is soothing, sweet, and life-giving to the heart of man. Have you taken the path of pride? Return and set foot on the path of humility, and despise pride, knowing that God opposes the proud. Have you taken the road of envy? Come back from this hellish path and be satisfied with what God has sent you, and remember: the first one to be envious was the devil, and *death entered the world by the envy of the devil* (Wis 2:24); be gracious unto all. If you have taken the path of hostility and anger, turn back and set foot on the road of meekness and love. Remember that *whoever hates his brother is a murderer* (1 John 3:15). Have you gone away from God through gluttony and

dissoluteness? Come back and take the path of sobri-
ety and chastity, and remember always to guide your
life by the words of the Saviour: *take heed to yourselves,
lest your hearts be weighed down with carousing, drunkenness, and cares of this life* (Luke 21:34), and the words of
the Prodigal Son: we have sinned before Thee and are
no longer worthy to be called Your sons; receive us, at least
as Your hired servants. And He will surely receive us as
His children. Amen.

HOMILY 4

On the Sunday of the Prodigal Son

Then he went and joined himself to a citizen of that country, and he sent him into his fields to feed the swine. And he would gladly have filled his stomach with the pods that the swine ate, and no one gave him anything. (Luke 15:15–16)

Behold what finally happened to the younger, prodigal son mentioned in today's Gospel parable, who did not, by his incomprehensible self-will, want to stay at his father's house, where, as he himself later acknowledged, even the *hired servants have bread enough and to spare* (Luke 15:17). Instead of being in his own home, and in the truly friendly company of his older, intelligent, well-behaved brother, he joined himself to some cruel citizen of that unfortunate country where he moved away from his father, and where he squandered his belongings living dissolutely. The oppressive citizen sent him into his fields to feed swine (Luke 15:15). Instead of the perfect contentment and abundance he had before in his father's house, now he suddenly endures extreme and shameful poverty, the fruits of a dissolute life, so much so that *he would gladly have filled his stomach with the pods*, or acorns, *that the swine ate* (Luke 15:16). This is how calamitous it was, brethren, for the prodigal son to move away from his father's house, with his share of the inheritance, into a strange and far away country!

Must we say that the prodigal son mentioned in the Holy Gospel is an image of us, sinners? More precisely, an image of our abilities: intellect, will, and heart, of body with its health, with its most wise and beautiful composition; of the vocation to which each one is called, of our wealth, of the entirety of our well-being, even the piece of land on which we live; all of this, the share of the goods of our Heavenly Father that have fallen to us, which He, solely out of His goodness, completely undeserved on our part, divided among each of us from his rich treasure and gave us the freedom to go in whichever of the four directions we wish to go. Rarely do any of us remain with his or her share under our father's roof; many of us, taking our share, move away from the All-good Father into a faraway country, into the sinful world, and live there dissolutely under the captivity of the passions, until, finally, their sheer oppression and destructiveness convince us to return to our Father's house. Yes, our passions, our sins are our tyrants. Let us discuss this.

The Lord our God is the most perfect Being, so much so that our intellect is not capable of grasping this idea. Just as He is all-perfect, He is also all-satisfied and all-blessed. The all-perfect and eternally blessed God created us not so that someone would torment or tyrannize us, but so that we would be eternally well, so that we would experience eternal bliss; however, because only he who strives for perfection and holiness, like God, can enjoy eternal bliss, the Creator also gave us free will, and commanded us to be holy, as He Himself is holy. *You shall be holy, for I the Lord your God am holy* (Lev 19:2; 1 Pet 1:16). Strive to imitate Him in holiness with your intellect, your will, and your senses; get to know His perfection, love Him and in Him love all people, perform the deeds of God, and you will be holy and blessed. If you will not strive to know Him, love Him, and do that which He commanded, then you will be a miserable sinner, a perpetual prisoner, a martyr of your own passions, because blessedness is in God and from God. Outside Him there can be no blessedness, there is only the tyrannical dominion of the passions.

What is it for man to know and love God with all his soul and all his heart?! If his soul were a creation alien to God ... but no, it is God's own creation, the breath of His lips, His image; how can it not love its own Creator, its own eternal Benefactor, completely and utterly?! Our body is the work of His all-wise Intellect, of

His creative hands; our calling, our wealth, all that we have, apart from sin, belongs to Him. How can we not know and love with all our soul such a Benefactor, Who *gives to all life, breath, and all things. for in Him we live and move and have our being* (Acts 17:25, 28). How can we not love one another, together with Him, as brothers, as children of one and the same Father! Is it fair to wonder how can we know and love anything else besides Him?! How can we move far away from Him, the Source of life and blessings, how can we rise up against His law and His statutes, how can we do anything that is not pleasing to Him?! Unfortunately, we love many other things instead of Him, and we do not do that which is pleasing to Him, and move away from Him. Take a look at what happens to us when we do this, look at who we sometimes resemble.

The audacious freethinker, who says not in his heart, but already with his lips proclaims that *there is no God* (Ps 14:1), or there is no God-Man, no Redeemer, there is no Church, there are no heavenly gifts, distributed in the mysteries for our spiritual life, our perfection, and salvation! What then? You repudiate all that is spiritual, heavenly, and holy? Thus you are flesh, earth, within you there is no soul, you don't want to know heaven, or hell, your eternal destination. Tell me, where is your soul? Every soul comes from God and knows Him, craves for Him, but for your soul there is no God, it doesn't know

Him; it's easier to say that your soul doesn't exist than that God, the Creator of all that exists, doesn't exist. Oh, I see what a pitiable thing it is that you call your soul. In an unknown distance from the Father of spirits and of all flesh it languishes, poor thing, in the realm of the flesh, of darkness and death, in inexpressible sorrow. It languishes for something lost, something akin to it... what emptiness and darkness it feels within, how bleak the condition in which it finds itself! To be a spirit, to have spiritual needs and desires and not to find any satisfaction for them, what a torment for the soul! It sees how other people rush to the churches of God offering diligent prayers to God, how they receive gifts of heavenly grace, and at the same time they feel within themselves the struggle of their proud intellect, which refuses to submit to holy truth together with the natural cravings of their soul: how destructive this is for the soul.

Return home, prodigal son: where did you go? Why do you squander the goods of your Heavenly Father away from Him, living dissolutely? Your intellect is not yours, it is a gift from God; why do you misuse it? God gave it to you so that you would know Him and would strive to be like Him; in the meantime you use it as a detrimental tool to move farther away from Him, to forget Him and not know Him. Return to your Father, you miserable being; you went far away; there is nothing but eternal death where you went.

Behold the ambitious man, for whom earthly honors are the goal of his life. Instead of striving for the eternal honor of the lofty calling in Jesus Christ, he exhausts all efforts to achieve as much acclaim as he can from people. However, on the way to his goal he meets many rivals who captivate merits that, according to his opinion, belong to him! How annoying, how difficult it is to not receive that for which you strive so diligently, and that you sometimes already believe belongs to you! How many nights the ambitious man spends without sleep! Return as well to your Father's house; do you not notice that you are going to a faraway country, farther and farther away from your Heavenly Father? *Friendship of the world*, love for its honors and dignity, *is enmity with God* (Jas 4:4). Why do you desire to be above others? Do you not know that *all the glory of man as the flower of grass. The grass withers. And the flower falls away* (1 Pet 1:24; Isa 40:6)? Do you not know that eternal glory is offered to us in heaven together with Christ? You were given a heart, in which, by the way, there is a burning love for good renown, not so that you would always aspire for transitory honors, but so that you would love the spiritual ascent from glory to glory, turning away every sin as the biggest obstacle to your spiritual perfection. Return to your father's house, forsake this small ambition.

Behold the lover of money, through whose hands already have passed many earthly coins, and who desires to gather them, the more the better. Silver and gold, those are his idols. And he moved away from God into a faraway country; the wearisome concerns regarding the acquisition and preservation of his wealth haunt him day and night. Sometimes he hears the word of God, but the thought of wealth suppresses it: he never has time to think of God, of his soul and its fate after death; and so he lives dissolutely. How much and what means he sometimes uses in order to acquire these beautiful, glittering pieces of earth, as much as can accommodate his unlimited desires! Where do you put it, why do you need so much silver and gold? Are you saving it for a rainy day, in order to provide for your family? But in the life of the true Christian there should be no rainy days, that is, unfortunate, dark days, according to secular understanding; dark days are those days in which we sin greatly and provoke the wrath of the All-good Master of our life.

We live in the kingdom of our most-loving and caring Father, of the eternal Mediator, the Son of God, and of the Consoler, the Holy Spirit—our God, the consubstantial Trinity. What dark days can there be in such a kingdom? You gathered all this money to provide for your family? All right. But in order to provide for one's family, is it necessary to gather, for example, no less than you did? And you wish to provide for the future of your family completely by yourself?! Why do you not allow God to provide for the future well-being of your children, but instead allow almost exclusively this dead metal to provide for them? And what if this shiny metal falls into the hands of wasteful and dissolute children? What if it spoils them? Then you will have twice the misery: first, because having gathered it, you did not use your wealth as you should have, and second, because you ruined your children. Return also to your Father's house.

You think that you increase the portion given to you from your Heavenly Father? No, you waste it by living dissolutely. To increase your share means to multiply it using it according to God's desire. How? To multiply it by using it? But, you may say, when you use it then you do not multiply it, but instead squander it. In the world it happens precisely like that, but not with God. However, you do not use it as you should, therefore you squander it, you squander it without fail, whether you want to or not. Perhaps, sometimes, you do it without even noticing it yourself. Return also to your Heavenly Father's house; know here that every earthly wealth belongs to Him, and that we are merely the administrators and distributors of this wealth; be certain that when we distribute our wealth to the poor as much as possible, we do not squander it, but acquire it.

Behold the slave of luxury and voluptuousness. What about him? Does he think about returning to his

Heavenly Father? Or have the torments of his soul and his physical suffering still not reached their breaking point? But why wait for that moment when the soul is completely paralyzed from shameful deeds, from sensuality, and the body is exhausted from such constant, deadly exertion? Have you forgotten, beloved brother, that your body and soul are not yours, but God's? Besides belonging completely to God, as the work of His hands, we were also redeemed from our sins by the price of the blood of the Son of God. Have you forgotten that you must *glorify God in your body and in your spirit, which are God's* (1 Cor 6:20). You have moved far away from God; you rarely come to church, you are ashamed of showing yourself before the All-holy God with your impurity. Cleanse yourself and return to the Heavenly Father: it is worse for you in the faraway country with the oppressive master of your shameful passions. Come to Me, the Heavenly Father and His beloved Son say to you: you will be well with Me. *Come to Me, all you who labor and are heavy laden, and I will give you rest. For My yoke is easy, and My burden is light* (Matt 11:28, 30). It is true, your passions do not give you anything to eat beside the pods the pigs ate; your pleasure is unhealthy, imaginary; come to Me: with Me all are satisfied, with Me *the hired servants have bread enough and to spare* (Luke 15:17).

And what about the miserable victim of his insatiable belly? The man who out of immoderate love for delectable food and drink consumes it in excess, is always physically and spiritually ill. Return as well, your Heavenly Father has been looking for you. He does not want for you to be lost forever, but that you be saved. He wants for you to become sober, and for you to become a spiritual man, pleasing to God, instead of a carnal and ungodly man. Hate to serve your flesh, love moderation which is as gold, be spiritual, and do not squander your portion received from the Heavenly Father, your physical and spiritual strength, by living dissolutely. May your Heavenly Father's eternal goodness serve for you as motivation to return to His embrace. Look at yourself: you practically only eat and drink, you are constantly immersed in sensual pleasures; meanwhile the Heavenly Father tolerates you on His earth, He shines His sun on you, and He doesn't take away from you the goods that are completely His. Like the barren fig tree, you should have been cut down and thrown into the fire a long time ago; meanwhile, you are still standing. Return: the Holy Church is waiting for you. You have long forgotten her, your Mother. And all this time she worries about you, as for her own child, worrying about how to save her disobedient child.

The Lord calls everyone now through the voice of His Holy Church, to come to His fatherly embrace, wanting to save all. Soon will come the days of fasting and repentance; let us all rush to cleanse ourselves from our sins and passions, in order to become new and spiritual people. Almost all of us live dissolutely, in a faraway country, in a sinful land, completely forgetful of our true and desired native land in heaven.

Oh, holy faith! Come to the aid of all those who are lost, say that we undoubtedly have another life beyond the grave, an eternal life, either blessed or filled with torments, depending on how each person lives on this earth: either like the faithful son of the Heavenly Father, in constant communion with God, in purity, holiness and love, or like the prodigal son, far away from God, in lusts and impurity. Say that *flesh and blood cannot inherit from the kingdom of God* (1 Cor 15:50). *Likewise you also reckon yourselves to be dead indeed to sin, but alive to God in Jesus Christ our Lord. Therefore do not let sin reign in your mortal body, that you should obey it in its lusts. And do not present your members as instruments of unrighteousness to sin: but present yourselves to God as being alive from the dead, and your members as instruments of righteousness to God. For sin shall not have dominion over you: for you are not under law but under grace* (Rom 6:11–14). *Therefore let us cast off the works of darkness, and let us put on the armor of light. Let us walk properly, as in the day, not in revelry and drunkenness, not in lewdness and lust, not in strife and envy. But put on the Lord Jesus Christ, and make not provision for the flesh, to fulfill its lusts* (Rom 13:12–14). Amen.

HOMILY 5

On the Sunday of the Prodigal Son

Father, I have sinned against heaven and before you.
(Luke 15:18)

Beloved brethren, who among us hasn't or doesn't work for sin every day, willingly or unwillingly, consciously or unconsciously, knowingly or unknowingly? Who has not angered the Lord, the infinite Truth and Love? Who has not been wounded by the blade of sin and has not felt the severity and sharpness of sin, a heavy embarrassment of the conscience, sorrow and distress, these common followers of sin? All of us, young and old alike, are sinners before God, and because of this are worthy of punishment and separation from God; and if the Lord, out of His infinite love and compassion toward fallen man, had not given him repentance and remission of sins for the sake of the sacrifice on the cross of His Only-Begotten Son, then all men would have descended into hell, into the place of eternal torment.

But, glory be to the All-good and wise God, Who gave repentance to sinners, and life eternal. A countless number of sinners have washed themselves through tears of repentance, have been justified and sanctified through the Most-Pure Blood of Jesus Christ, the Lamb of God Who took our sins upon Himself and suffered for them all of the punishment that had been prepared for us, and now they rejoice with the angels in the mansions of the saints. All of you here present, sinners like me, do you treasure this priceless gift of the Lord, the gift of repentance? Do you sigh like the publican, do you cry like the prostitute, do you wash your beds with your tears, like our forefather David? Do you return to the Heavenly Father with sincere and deep repentance, as did the Prodigal Son, about whom we have listened in today's Gospel reading?

There is no other way for sinners to regain the grace and mercy of the Heavenly Father than the way of sincere and true repentance, together with the fruits of repentance. And the Holy Church, the bearer and interpreter of the Spirit of Christ, His infinite love and compassion, calls each and every one of us to repentance every day, and in the present days, due to the approaching great days of fasting and repentance, the Church calls us especially, by appointing as the Gospel reading for today's Sunday the Lord's touching parable about the Prodigal Son, as well as the contrite hymns of repentance. As good children, let us answer the tender, loving voice of our Holy Mother Church; let us awake from the sleep of sin, *let us walk properly, as in the day* (Rom 13:13); let us leave the lusts of the flesh, let us care for our immortal souls, let us begin to perform the works of the Lord; and then let us delight in the peace of soul and the consolation of a pure conscience. How merciful and quick to hear is our Father, our Master and Judge, God! He immediately hurries with His abundant mercies to every sinner who repents sincerely, saving him from troubles, sorrows, and dangers that result from sin, giving him peace and openness of heart, turning sorrow into joy. Every sinner who has sincerely repented has experienced this; and this is what today's Gospel reading about the prodigal, repentant son shows us.

As soon as he firmly resolved to return in repentance to his father's house and went, *his father saw him and had compassion, and ran and fell on his neck and kissed him. And the son said to him: 'Father! I have sinned against heaven and in your sight, and am no longer worthy to be called your son.' But the father said to his servants: 'Bring out the best robe and put it on him, and put a ring on his hands and sandals on his feet. And bring the fatted calf here and kill it, and let us eat and be merry, for this my son was dead and is alive again; he was lost and is found.' And they began to be merry* (Luke 15:20–25). A touching image of fatherly love on one hand, and on the other, sincere repentance.

This is a parable in which are presented the father, a good and merciful man, and his son, dissolute and repentant. But hearken to the deeper, inner meaning of this parable; imagine instead of an ordinary father, God, the Father of all mankind, and His limitless love toward the world that has fallen in sin. Which banquet did He prepare for sinners who He adopted through faith and baptism?

He did not kill a calf, but gave His Only-Begotten Son to voluntary slaughter; He did not prepare the flesh of a bullock for the feast, but the Body and Blood of His Son, which He gave and gives us as food and drink, for the remission of sins and life everlasting. Behold the spiritual, life-giving, wonderful, saving banquet of faith and salvation! Behold the limitless Fatherly love toward us, sinners! Do you, a sinner, feel this love? Do you respond to this love also with love? Do you repent sincerely of your transgressions, in order that you may also be worthy of the spiritual banquet for your salvation, and to delight in the love of the Heavenly Father, His Only-Begotten Son, and the Holy Spirit, the Comforter? Without repentance you will not have this mystery of salvation. And what are the best garments, the ring on his finger, and shoes on his feet? The best garments with which the father dressed his prodigal son represent the garment of righteousness, with which Jesus Christ vests us; or Christ Himself, as it is written: *For as many of you as were baptized into Christ have put on Christ* (Gal 3:27). This means that we must live in all righteousness and truth.

What does the ring on his finger represent? It represents the engagement of the Holy Spirit, which takes place in the hearts of believers. *Do you not know that you are the temple of God and that the Spirit of God dwells in you?* (1 Cor 3:16). The temple of God should be sanctified every day: let us lead holy lives. The shoes on his feet are the grace to walk right along the path of Christ's commandments: *Direct my steps*, it is said, *by Your word. And let no iniquity have dominion over me* (Ps 119:133), for without the shoes of grace we cannot walk the right paths of God's commandments. *Repent now everyone of his evil way and his evil doings* (Jer 25:5), says the word of God. And so, clad with spiritual shoes, let us hasten to God with spiritual zeal, laying aside the sleep of sin, laziness, and negligence. Soon Great Lent will be upon us; a time for preparation, confession of sins, and the communion of the holy and life-giving Mysteries; let us purify our souls and bodies through fasting, prayer, and sincere repentance, and transform ourselves into temples for the Lord, Who desires to come and abide in us.

Look at how those who desire to meet a king or an important person prepare themselves for such a meeting. They straighten and clean all the roads through which he will pass, they adorn their houses with flags, or lights, of different colors, and display all possible signs of zeal and joy; all try to see him and to look upon him, and if anyone was fortunate enough to receive the king in his house, then such a person would be beside himself with joy. If those who desire to meet an earthly king, who is himself a man, prepare themselves, meet and receive him thus, then you and I, who are preparing ourselves to meet the Heavenly King, Creator, and God, with how much more care and diligence must we prepare ourselves to receive Him? For as the Heavenly King is infinitely higher and more righteous than the earthly king, that much more diligent and better should be the preparation than the preparation to meet an earthy king. For the Heavenly King requires our souls and bodies to be pure and adorned with virtues, and not majestically ornamented houses, nor colorful flags; he requires a variety of virtues according to the capabilities and state of each person; he does not require burning lights, but requires our souls to be burning with love and faith. Let us all prepare ourselves to meet the Heavenly King, so that we might be granted the joy of receiving Him in our spiritual homes, in our hearts. Amen.

On Meatfare Sunday

I believe in the Lord Jesus Christ who will come in glory to judge the living and the dead. (7th article of the Symbol of Faith)

Who says these words? Every Christian does. Well, if every Christian says these words, then, without a doubt, so do I, and each and every one of you. Therefore, brothers and sisters, do you sincerely believe that Jesus Christ, the Righteous Judge of all those born on this earth, will come to judge the living and the dead, who will all be resurrected and receive either eternal blessedness or eternal damnation? Are you ready to meet the Judge of all and to give an answer at the terrible judgment seat of Christ for your every word and deed? Do you have any good deeds? Why do I keep asking? From the lives and deeds of Christians it is evident that they have long forgotten about the Righteous Judge, about the terrible judgment, about eternal life, and that with each passing day they rush toward eternal perdition, which they cannot even imagine. They hurry to receive their consolation here on earth, in order to be deprived of it in eternity, in heaven. They are more concerned with how to kill precious time, how to spend time in a pleasant way; but no one is concerned with how to spend time for the benefit of the soul, no one is concerned about preparing their *outside work. Making it fit for* themselves *in the field* (Prov 24:27).

Those who desire eternal joys partake little of earthly ones (St Gennadius, "On the Christian Faith and Life"), says St Gennadius, Patriarch of Constantinople, and yet our earthly joys are almost uninterrupted. Many of us live as if we don't have to die and give an account of our lives. What does this mean? Doesn't this happen because such people think that all they have to do is to repent just before they die and they will receive a full pardon? Of course, God does not turn away those who come to him even at the eleventh hour, that is, if they turn to him with all their hearts. However, if your heart was far away from God for the longest part of your life, do you think that you will be able to move it toward God, to arouse in you a feeling of repentance before you die? Oh, brothers! It will be exactly then that your heart will be set against you, for your perdition. Many times have I seen how difficult it is for some to listen to an exhortation to repentance, and how those who never thought about correcting themselves, and were not able to repent during their lives, how they are lost during confession before their departure from this life. No, brothers! A Christian ending is a reward for true Christians. Repent as much as you can during your lifetime, and then you will meet a peaceful death with sincere repentance.

Therefore, prepare yourselves for the judgment, for the terrible judgment, for the righteous judgment, for the one and final judgment, after which there will be either eternal blessedness or unending torment. Do not be surprised that I speak so emphatically. Truth is royal, it has the right to speak thusly. Moreover, we have the utmost need to speak emphatically about the preparation for the judgment. When we are clearly confronted with the eternal perdition of souls due to carelessness and negligence, then we must act decisively, and then even more decisively than at other times when we must speak the truth. When people see that a man faces a clear risk of death by fire, or by drowning in water, then in such cases do they not act with all determination? Yes, because in the case of indecision on the part of those who want to save the man who is perishing, he could die at any moment. In the same way we must, with great determination and fear of the coming judgment, save many from the fire: because we ourselves are not far from the eternal fire, and perhaps many people are but one step away from it. Brother! Think, maybe *this night your soul will be required of you* (Luke 12:20), and you will be in hell, in torments ... all in flames. Thus, be prepared for the judgment, start preparing today. *Work the works of Him who sent Me while it is day: the night is coming when no one can work* (John 9:4). We have worked for vanity long enough. It is time to look upon our poor soul with testing eyes.

Go to Church, weep over your sins, await together with Her, with great fear, the day of judgment. The Church continually thinks about the judgment: morning, day, and night; every day, early and late, the Church reminds Her children of this great day, which will decide the fate of the entire human race; and yet Her children are busy with thoughts of how pleasant it is for them to turn their heads for a few minutes, to cheer their hearts with the joys of earthly passions. The Lord, the Truth, the Life thunders with His voice about how His Judgment will be accomplished without fail, and commands us to *watch and pray* always in spirit (Mark 13:33; Luke 21:36), in order that we may avoid the terrible fate of the condemned; the Apostles assure us that *the Judge is standing at the door* (Jas 5:9) ... and we act as if we don't even want to hear any of this. Others think and even say: what a terrible judgment! The Lord is merciful, He will have compassion; we are sinners more due to our weaknesses, not because we are evil or callous.... And they do not think about how only the merciful *shall obtain mercy*

(Matt 5:7). *For judgment is without mercy to the one who has shown no mercy* (Jas 2:13). Where are your deeds of mercy, when it is evident that you care only about yourselves?

Brethren! God forbid that any of us go to where the rich man, who made merry every day, went. If we find ourselves there, then it will be too late to ask for drops of water to sooth our tongue; it will be too late to send anyone to our relatives, in order that they might not end there also (Luke 16:19–31).

Watch therefore, for you know neither the day nor the hour in which the Son of Man is coming (Matt 25:13). Amen.

HOMILY 7

On Meatfare Sunday

Beloved in the Lord, my brothers and sisters! Today we have read in the Gospel of Matthew the words of our Lord Jesus Christ regarding His second, glorious, and terrible coming to earth; we read about how He will sit on the throne of His glory in order to judge the world, and how all nations shall be gathered before Him, everyone, those whose lives have passed, those who now live, and those who have yet to be born. *And He will separate them one from another, as a shepherd divides his sheep from the goats. And He will set the sheep on His right hand, but the goats on the left. Then the King will say to those on His right hand, 'Come, you blessed of My Father, inherit the kingdom prepared for you from the foundation of the world: for I was hungry and you gave Me food: I was thirsty and you gave Me drink: I was a stranger and you took Me in: I was naked and you clothed Me: I was sick and you visited Me: I was in prison and you came to Me.' Then the righteous will answer Him, saying, 'Lord, when did we see You hungry and feed You, or thirsty and give You drink? When did we see You a stranger and take You in, or naked and clothe You? Or when did we see You sick, or in prison, and come to You?' And the King will answer and say to them, 'Assuredly, I say to you, inasmuch as you did it to one of the least of these My brethren, you did it to Me.' Then He will also say to those on the left hand, 'Depart from me, you cursed, into the everlasting fire prepared for the devil and his angels: for I was hungry and you gave Me no food: I was thirsty and you gave Me no drink: I was a stranger and you did not take Me in, naked and you did not clothe Me, sick and in prison and you did not visit Me.' Then they also will answer Him, saying, 'Lord, when did we see You hungry or thirsty or a stranger or naked or sick or in prison, and did not minister to You?' Then He will answer them, saying, 'Assuredly, I say to you, inasmuch as you did not do it to one of the least of these, you did not do it to Me.' And these will go away into everlasting punishment, but the righteous into life eternal* (Matt 25:32–46).

This is how the Lord concluded His words on the final, terrible judgment of mankind! How sweet and joyful these words sound to the righteous and how bitter and stern, and forever unchanging they sound to hard-hearted sinners! Thus, the merciful *shall obtain mercy* (Matt 5:7). Those who have stored the oil of good deeds will be able to enter the bridal chamber, *for judgment is without mercy to the one who has shown no mercy* (Jas 2:13).

Now, brothers and sisters, it is beneficial for us to ask ourselves and to ponder: to which side shall we belong? To the right, or to the left; with the sheep, or with the goats; with the blessed, or with the cursed? You will say: who can know such a thing, besides the Lord, *Who saves the upright in heart* (Ps 7:10), and Who possesses the most truthful scales of justice? To the Lord alone belongs the perfect knowledge regarding every man, only He knows who among us will stand on the right side, and who will stand on the left side; He alone knows which righteous person shall stand here in his righteousness, and which one won't, which sinner returns sincerely and repents, and from a goat is turned into a sheep, and which one ultimately becomes hardened in sin.

But to us, brethren, is given at least to know what is our state now: who are we, sheep or goats? Our conscience, that incorruptible judge and witness of our thoughts, words, and deeds, shows us whether we are humble and gentle sheep of the rational fold, whether we are willing to share our goods with those in need, or whether we are proud, egotistical, evil, vengeful, unmerciful sinners, who, like goats, are filled with the stench of our impurities. This we can know about ourselves right here and now, in the continuation of our earthly lives, and therefore we can judge on which side we might stand at the terrible judgment; that is, we might stand on the left side if we remain unrepentant, uncorrected sinners, filled with our pride and malice, with sinful impurities in our hearts and bodies; yet we may hope that through faith, repentance, and good deeds, we might stand on the right side; the choice of which side to stand on depends on us. Time was given to each of us by the merciful Saviour to come to our senses, repent, correct ourselves, stock up with an excess of oil of mercy and every virtue, in order not to be ashamed at the judgment. Thus, let us take care to become lambs of meekness and gentleness, love and compassion, patience and long-suffering, humility and obedience, temperance and purity, and let us flee all the opposites of these virtues. The aforesaid virtues attain for us in this life the blessings of the Heavenly Father, and in the future life they establish us on the right side.

Therefore I repeat, it is up to us to become worthy to stand on the right side at the dreadful judgment, and to flee the left side; to listen to the all-blessed voice of the Saviour, Who calls us into the Kingdom of Heaven, and to flee the terrible voice that casts us into the eternal fire.

We write here, as it were, our deeds, eternal justification or eternal condemnation for ourselves at the terrible judgment; and in this way we say that the future judgment is written: *to execute on them*, it is said, *the written judgment* (Ps 149:9). The books of our consciences either justify us or condemn us, and all that is left to us is to listen to the just, eternal sentence of the Judge of all. Let us hasten, through sincere repentance and charity, to obliterate from our consciences all of our sins, voluntary and involuntary, and to write in our consciences every good deed. *Their works follow them* (Rev 14:13), says the Scripture. Amen.

HOMILY 8

On Cheesefare Sunday

When you fast, do not be like the hypocrites, with a sad countenance. For they disfigure their faces that they may appear to men to be fasting. (Matt 6:16)

In our times there are very few people who would like to hypocritically appear to be great fasters in order to be praised by other people. It is much easier today to find people who neither desire to fast nor to appear to be fasting because they think fasting is useless and futile, and that to appear to be fasting so as to be noticed by others is foolish and ridiculous. However, between such extremes, there are certainly those among Christians who try to follow the golden mean, deviating neither right nor left, and follow the path of fasting directly and precisely, as true fasters, keeping a good fast, well-pleasing to the Lord.

Tomorrow begins the Great Forty Day Fast, or Great Lent, a time truly precious for people who are able to

46

fast as it should be done, in a Christian spirit. So that this time will be profitable for our souls and bring us salvation, let us now talk about the need for the fast and its benefits.

Is fasting necessary, that is, abstaining not only from non-fasting foods but also abstaining from food in large quantities? Is fasting necessary, that is, abstaining from the pleasures of our crude sensuality? Is fasting necessary, that is, abstaining from improper thoughts and movements of the heart, as well as blameworthy actions? And do you, beloved, wish to inherit eternal bliss, or the kingdom of heaven, which surely exists, as surely as now we live on this earth, as the incarnate Word of God Himself assures us, as do His Prophets, Apostles, and all His Saints? How can we not desire this?! There, according to the true and immutable Word of God, live eternally *righteousness and peace and joy in the Holy Spirit* (Rom 14:17); God is there, as are the blessed spirits and righteous people; but on earth, in the course of only some seventy years, almost all you see are sins, confusion, and misery everywhere. If you desire (eternal bliss and the kingdom of heaven), then you must necessarily fast, as *flesh and blood cannot inherit the kingdom of God* (1 Cor 15:50), *for the kingdom of God is not eating and drinking* (Rom 14:17).

Flesh and blood, meat and drink, being things that are crude, elementary, earthly, must remain on earth and undergo the same fate of all things earthly—that is, corruption. In heaven there is not and there cannot be a place for crude flesh and blood, namely because there is heaven, not earth, and beings of that world possess spiritual, luminous properties completely different from those of people living among earthly lusts. Shall I speak to you about God Himself, the Father of all blessed inhabitants of heaven? He is the purest Spirit, Who abhors the affairs of the flesh as being defiled, outside the boundaries of the law, of moderation and decency. *My Spirit shall not strive with man forever*, said He regarding people who insulted Him by their attachment to sensual pleasures. Why? *For he is indeed flesh*, He said (Gen 6:3); because they are rough flesh, a piece of earth, in which there is nothing spiritual, akin to Myself. See how He now also speaks regarding us: My Spirit cannot remain with these people, because they are burly flesh, in which My Spirit cannot abide, for in them abides sin and impurity, whereas I am righteous and holy.

Shall I speak now about the created spirits? They are the holiest beings after God, who are also pure and holy, strangers to all that is material, and who can receive within their blessed company only those who throw off from themselves the yoke of slavery to carnal things, and who, while living on earth, think of heaven, and do not serve the whims of their flesh, knowing that with time it will be reduced to dust.

Shall I speak of the holy men of God, who have gone from this perishable earth into the eternal heavenly mansions? They are earthly angels, who due to their fasting and vigils, martyrdom and various virtues, rose above their own flesh and made their nature so worthy that the bodies of many of them, having partaken of divine grace, rose above the common fate of all that is material, that is, corruption. They knew that our body is a home built by the hands of a skilled artisan, in which a being of heavenly origin lives only temporarily, who must after a short time leave his earthly tabernacle and soar back to its place; because of this they lived not for the body, but for the spirit. Yes, in order to make our life blessed, the Lord was pleased to place us in this world; but only for a short time, so that, having enjoyed the earth, and contemplating on earth all of the material creations of God, heavenly and earthly, their beauty, precision, the orderliness in their various, countless multitude, we would love their creator and would desire to be united to Him, the Origin of all beauty, and through deeds of holiness and love we would earn here on earth this eternal union.

It is as if He told each person here on earth who contemplates His creation: See how My creation is immense, and yet at the same time how it is precise and beautiful. Look upon yourself, how small and insignificant you are within My creation, and yet I promise you, tiny being, the heavens, with their boundlessness and infinitude, as your inheritance; I promise it to you on certain conditions, and you know that I am the Truth, and therefore I cannot lie. Why do you not try to fulfill these conditions? Why do you cling to the earth, and with such strength that you cannot tear away from it? Is it possible you do not want to come to Me, then, so that united to Me, the Creator of everything you see, you may receive eternal pleasure from the knowledge and contemplation of My countless creations, and even more than this, to be blessed in Me, the source of bliss for all rational creatures? How can your soul not soar to heaven, not *abstain from fleshly lusts which war against the soul* (1 Pet 2:11); how can your soul not take precedence over your sin-loving flesh, which pulls you down to earth, and which in time will lie in it, like a lump of earth? What benefit do you receive from dainty food and drink, how are you not ashamed to burden yourself with them? Why do you submit yourself to the rule of sensuality? Is this pleasing to you? Look, the imaginary sweetness of your pleasures is a dangerous lure of the flesh, through which it easily gains preponderance over your soul and does not allow you to think of heaven and strive for it. Fear this lure. Like a fly in honey, you will get stuck in it and remain there until you die.

Is the fast necessary, as a means to abstain from improper thoughts and movements of the heart, as well as blameworthy actions? If you agree that God is your

Law-Giver and just Judge, Who knows how to punish those who transgress His laws; if your conscience tells you that your soul upset the order of moral life, disobeying the laws of the Creator, then you must agree that you need to restore the order of your moral life, bring your thoughts from their random agitation to and fro back to their proper order, force your heart to break away from unworthy goals, to which it has clung so strongly due to your carelessness and negligence, that it has forgotten the first object of its love, God; you must behave so that your actions would not be shameful if exposed before the judgment of your conscience and the judgment of people and of God. You know that a sinful thought is an abomination to God, that God requires your heart, which you willingly submitted to the passions, for Himself, and that the impure and *the boastful shall not stand in* His *sight* (Ps 5:5). If you wish to be united with God, if you desire eternal bliss, then you must agree that it behooves you to fast with your soul, gather your mind, correct your thoughts, purify them, and instead of wearing the rags of iniquitous deeds you must adorn yourself with the precious garment of good deeds. The physical fast was established to facilitate the fasting of the spirit.

Shall I, even after this, speak of the benefits of the fast, seeing as how when we spoke of its necessity, we already have partially mentioned its benefits? The fast pacifies our sinful, capricious flesh, freeing it from the weight of the soul, conferring it wings, as it were, so it can soar toward the heavens, providing a place for the action of God's grace. He who fasts freely and correctly knows how the soul becomes free and bright during the fast; then good thoughts easily enter the heart, the heart becomes purer, more tender, more compassionate; we feel an inclination toward good deeds; compunction for our sins appears in our souls, which start to feel the deadliness of the state we are in and start to grieve over its sins.

When we do not fast, on the other hand, when our thoughts are in disarray, when our heart is unrestrained and our will allows us everything, then rarely can you see a saving change in man, then his soul is dead: all of its forces act in the wrong direction; the main purpose for his actions, the meaning of life, leaves his sight, and in its place many other particular goals appear, almost as many as there are passions or whims inside each man. A strange activity happens within the soul, and its result seems to be some sort of building up. You see the materials needed for the construction, the beginning, middle, and end of the work, but in fact it comes to nothing. The soul acts against itself, against its own salvation, with all its powers: intellect, will, and the senses. He who fasts as a Christian should, rationally, freely, becomes worthy, according to the true promise of the Lord, of receiving a reward from the Heavenly Father for his ascetical efforts. *Your Father*, said the Saviour to the true faster, *Who sees in secret will Himself reward you openly* (Matt 6:4). And this reward, without a doubt, is always generous, truly fatherly, serving for our most essential benefit.

Brethren! Let us understand that our body is the temple of the Holy Spirit, and that we do not belong to ourselves, but to God, because we have been bought for the price of the Blood of the Son of God. *Or do you not know that your body is the temple of the Holy Spirit who is in you, whom you have from God, and you are not your own? For you were bought at a price* (1 Cor 6:19–20). Let us respect our nature, elevated through its participation in the divine nature; let us eat and drink only as much as is necessary to sustain our life and strengthen our forces; let us not submit our nature to the power of impure passions, but let us make it holy, something we ourselves would not be ashamed to look at, and in which God could recognize the work of His hands. Until now we have sinned and given ourselves over to the pleasures of our rough sensuality. Let us at least now live chastely and in a holy manner; until now we had been away from God due to our carnal deeds, let us at least now draw near to Him, and know how good He is. Look, He gives us His Body and Blood as food. If you are convinced that by yourself, without God, you are nothing more than unclean rot, ashes, a sinner, a stranger to a grace-filled life, then you will understand what a great blessing it is for the Lord to nourish us with His Body and Blood. He is the source of life for all creatures, and He desires to establish within you, through union with Him in the mystery of communion, His life, His perfection, His peace, His blessedness, and to make you live forever. Let us always keep in mind that our soul must strive toward God-like perfection, toward precious freedom of the soul, and that it cannot achieve this perfection if we make it earthly through carnal deeds, binding it with the tight and heavy chains of materialism.

May the Lord help us meet the fast with joy. Amen.

On Cheesefare Sunday

For if you forgive men their trespasses, your heavenly Father will also forgive you. (Matt 6:14)

The present Sunday is called among the Russian Orthodox people Forgiveness Sunday, from the good and pious custom to forgive one another, that is, to ask forgiveness of one another before Great Lent. This custom originated from the Saviour's commandment, read in today's Gospel, to forgive one another if we want our sins to be forgiven by our Heavenly Father, Whom we offend countless times and Whose wrath we provoke every day and hour.

Let us repeat once again the Gospel that was read today: The Lord says: *For if you forgive men their trespasses, your heavenly Father will also forgive you. But if you do not forgive men their trespasses, neither will your Father forgive your trespasses. Moreover, when you fast, do not be like the hypocrites, with a sad countenance.*

For they disfigure their faces that they may appear to men to be fasting. Assuredly, I say to you, they have their reward. But you, when you fast, anoint your head and wash your face, so that you do not appear to men to be fasting, but to your Father who is in the secret place, and your Father who sees in secret will reward you openly. Do not lay up for yourselves treasures on earth, where moth and rust destroy and where thieves break in and steal; but lay up for yourselves treasures in heaven, where neither moth nor rust destroys and where thieves do not break in and steal. For where your treasure is, there your heart will be also (Matt 6:14–21). With these words ends the Gospel reading appointed for this Sunday.

Since Great Lent starts tomorrow, and all of us, according to the Christian custom, are preparing to throw off the heavy burden of our sins, and seeing how this act of throwing off the burden of sin requires some self-sacrifice on our part, as well as some skill, the Lord teaches us what exactly is required of us in order that our sins be completely forgiven, or what we must do on our part, since the Lord God, on His part, is always ready to save and have mercy on repentant sinners. The Lord says that simplicity is required of us, as well as the absence of rancor and wrath; it is required that we forget offenses and possess friendliness and love for our enemies. Your salvation is in your hands, within your power. If you will forgive others their offenses, sins, their nuisance and constant requests, then your sins will be forgiven, and you, with your own nuisance and constant requests to God, will never go away from Him empty-handed, and will receive from Him great and abundant mercies. If you forgive the sins of your neighbor, which compared to your sins against God are few, then God will forgive your countless shortcomings; you forgive the debt of one hundred pence, and the Lord forgives your debt of many talents. But what rancor people often possess! Then, the Lord requires little of us—that we forgive and forget other's offenses—which are like drops in the ocean when compared to our sins against God, and requires this for our own benefit and desires to teach us meekness, gentleness, patience, humble-mindedness, brotherly love, forbearance, peace; in the meantime we are beside ourselves, showing which of our rights have been violated by our neighbors, kindling within ourselves and in our neighbors the flames of enmity, and in this way we madly and boldly push away from ourselves the saving hand of God, adding sin to sin, and rushing headlong toward destruction. Gentleness before God and our neighbors is a great blessing and a great virtue; it covers a multitude of sins. Abel, Abraham, Isaac, Jacob, Moses, David, the ancestor of God, king and prophet, and many other people in the Old Testament were especially loved and glorified by God for having this virtue. In the New Testament, a countless number of saints imitated the meek and humble Lord, God and Saviour Jesus Christ, who told all of us in the Gospel: *learn from Me, for I am gentle and lowly in heart: and you will find rest for your souls* (Matt 11:29). Therefore, let us not listen to the devil, who teaches us to feed the evil against our neighbor, but let us, in simplicity of heart, forgive the offenses caused by our neighbors, also at the instigation of the enemy. Let no one think evil against one another; let no one be distracted by evil suspicions against his neighbor, for all of these are the illusions of the enemy of our salvation, who tries in every possible way to destroy the bonds of love in us and to sow demonic hatred and hostility. Let us remember the Saviour's commandment: *A new commandment I give to you, that you love one another* (John 13:34), and the words of the Apostle Paul: *for he who loves another has fulfilled the law.* Therefore, *love is the fulfillment of the law* (Rom 13:8, 10).

Then the Lord teaches us how to observe the fast without hypocrisy, so that we enter the arena of the fast not with sad faces, but with joyous ones, as true and faithful warriors of Christ, who enter the struggle against sin and our much-passionate flesh with the help and assistance of the omnipotent grace of Christ, and before the face of the Heavenly Father, Who is prepared to reward all those who truly struggle against the deceptions of sin. *Anoint your head*, says the Saviour, *and wash your face* (Matt 6:17), that is, anoint your soul with the oil of alms, and wash the face of your soul with the oil of purity, and your Father *who sees in secret will reward you openly* (Matt 6:18).

Later the Lord teaches us to turn our hearts away from earthly treasures and earthly passions, and encourages us to desire and look for heavenly treasures; first, because our souls have their origin in heaven and are immortal, whereas earthly goods, being gross, perishable, and transient, are not worthy of us, who were created and redeemed by the Blood of the Son of God in order to enjoy spiritual and eternal blessedness. Second, because if our hearts cling to earthly goods they also become earthly, gross, lowly, passionate, and we become incapable of loving God and our neighbor, whereas love is the main purpose and responsibility of our lives. *Do not lay up for yourselves treasures upon earth, where moth and rust destroy and where thieves break in and steal, but lay up for yourselves treasures in heaven, where neither moth nor rust destroys and where thieves do not break in and steal. For where your treasure is, there will your heart be also* (Matt 6:19–21). St John Chrysostom speaks eloquently about this in the following way: you will undergo no small harm, in being bound to the things below, and in becoming a slave instead of a freeman, and casting yourself out of the heavenly things, and having no power to think on anything that is high, but all about money, usuries and loans, and gains, and ignoble traffickings.

What could be more wretched than this? For in truth such a one will be worse off than any slave, bringing upon himself a most grievous tyranny, and giving up the most important thing of all, the nobility and liberty of man. No matter how much anyone will talk to you; you will not be able to hear what really concerns you because your mind is bound to money: *for where your treasure is, there your heart will be also*. While laying up treasure in heaven by means of alms you will not only reap heavenly honors, those fruits of your labors, but also in this world you will receive a reward through lifting up your mind to heaven, concerning yourself and thinking about the heavenly. For is it obvious that you have set your mind on heaven and placed your treasure there. You will experience completely the opposite if you lay up for yourself treasure on the earth (Comment on the Gospel of Matt 6:31).

Therefore, let us take to heart the advice of our Saviour, offered to us in today's Gospel regarding the forgiveness of offenses, regarding a God-pleasing fast, the detachment of our hearts from earthly treasures and loving incorruptible, heavenly blessings. Using the words of St John Chrysostom, let us prepare ourselves for our departure from here. Even though the day in which everything will end is not yet upon us, still, the end for each one of us, old and young, is already at the doors....

So, while we still have time, let us prepare our boldness before God; let us stock up abundantly on oil, let us store all our treasures in heaven, so that when our time comes, and when we will have need of these things, we may enjoy them, through the grace and love for mankind of our Lord Jesus Christ, to Whom is due all glory and dominion, now and ever, and to the ages of ages. Amen.

On Cheesefare Sunday

For if you forgive men their trespasses, your heavenly Father will also forgive you. But if you do not forgive men their trespasses, neither will your Father forgive your trespasses, says the Lord. (Matt 6:14–15)

The present Sunday is called colloquially Forgiveness Sunday because today we read the passage from the Gospel that commands us to forgive the trespasses of our neighbors against us, so that our Heavenly Father may also forgive our countless transgressions. Therefore, since ancient times, it is the custom of pious Christians on this day, and all throughout Cheesefare week, to ask forgiveness of one another for any faults we might have committed against our neighbors. This is a beautiful, truly Christian custom because who among us does not sin against his neighbor in word, deed, or thought? And by asking forgiveness of one another, we show our faith in the Gospel, our humility, our gentleness and love of peace; and on the contrary, the lack of desire to ask forgiveness from those against whom we are really to blame shows lack of faith in reconciliation, pride, conceit, rancor, disobedience to the Gospel, opposition to God, and compliance with the devil.

All of us are children of the Heavenly Father according to grace, we are members of the Body of Christ, members of the single body of the Church, which is His Body, and we are members of one another; *God is love* (1 John 4:8), and He requires from us, more than all burnt offerings and sacrifices, mutual love that *suffers long and is kind; love does not envy; love does not parade itself, is not puffed up; does not behave rudely, does not seek its own, is not provoked, thinks no evil; does not rejoice in iniquity, but rejoices in the truth; bears all things, believes all things, hopes all things, endures all things. Love never fails* (1 Cor 13:4–8). All of the Law of God is comprised in these words: love God and neighbor. Meanwhile, the human heart is extremely selfish, impatient, capricious, evil, and rancorous; it is ready to be angry at our neighbor not only for any direct offense but also for imaginary ones; not only because of an offensive word but also because of any unpleasant, or truthful, or sharp word; even by an opinion that may seem unkind, or ambiguous, evil, or proud; the heart is ready to become angry even at our neighbor's thoughts, which we imagine he may have. Our Lord, Who looks into the heart of man, spoke thus about the heart of man: *For from within, out of the heart of men, proceed evil thoughts, adulteries, fornications, murders, thefts, covetousness, wickedness, deceit, lewdness, an evil eye, blasphemy, pride, foolishness* (Mark 7:21–22).

However, against a strong infirmity, there must also be powerful means; the great wickedness of man opposed to the infinite goodness and all-powerful grace of God: with its help it is possible to overcome any evil within oneself and in others—meekness, gentleness, acquiescence, patience, and longsuffering. *But I tell you*, says the Lord, *not to resist an evil person. But whoever slaps you on your right cheek, turn the other to him also. If anyone wants to sue you and take away your tunic, let him have your cloak also* (Matt 5:39–40). If we forgive the sins of our neighbors, our Heavenly Father has promised to forgive us our own sins, to have mercy on us at the terrible judgment, and eternal blessedness: the merciful *shall obtain mercy* (Matt 5:7). However, irreconcilable wickedness is threatened by the just judgment of God and eternal torment. Listen to a story that shows how God punishes people still in this life who remain bitter and irreconcilable with each other.

In the Kiev Caves Lavra, in ancient times, there were two monks, the priest Titus and the deacon Evagrius. Having lived amicably with one another for several years, for some reason they developed enmity and hatred toward one another; this mutual anger continued for a very long time, and they, not having reconciled with one another, dared to offer the Bloodless Sacrifice to God. No matter how much the brethren advised them to leave aside all anger and to live in peace and harmony with one another, all was in vain. One day, the priest Titus fell gravely ill. Despairing for his life, he began to sorely grieve over his sins, and sent for his foe in order to ask for his forgiveness; however, Evagrius not only did not want to hear any of it, he also started to harshly curse him. The brethren, feeling sorry for such a grave error, forcibly brought him to the dying brother. Seeing his enemy, Titus, with the help of the brethren, got up from his bed and fell at his feet, tearfully begging his forgiveness. Nonetheless, Evagrius was so inhumane that he turned his back on him and exclaimed furiously: "neither in this life, nor in the future one, do I want to be reconciled with him!" He broke free from the hands of the brethren, and fell to the ground.

The monks wanted to raise him up, but they were astonished to see that he was dead, and so cold, as if he had been dead for a long time already. Their amazement increased all the more when, at the same time, Titus the priest got up from his bed of sickness healthy, as if he had never been ill. Terrified at such an extraordinary event, they surrounded Titus and one after another they asked him: "What does this mean?" He answered: "While I was gravely ill, I, a sinner, still angry with my brother, saw how the angels were leaving my side and were lamenting over the death of my soul, and how the unclean spirits were rejoicing; this was the reason I wanted to be reconciled with him more than anything. But as soon as he was brought over here and I prostrated myself before him, and he started to curse me, I saw how one terrible angel struck him with a flaming spear, and he, an unfortunate one, fell dead on the floor. This same angel gave me his hand and raised me from the bed of infirmity." The monks mourned over the cruel death of Evagrius, and from that day on, more than ever, they began to guard themselves, so that they never let the sun go down upon their wrath.

Brothers and sisters! Rancor is a terrible vice, and as it is disgusting before God, so it is detrimental to society. We are made according to the image and likeness of God; meekness and gentleness must be our immutable features, for God always acts toward us according to His meekness; He suffers us and forgives us countlessly. And so we must also forgive others. A rancorous person does not possess in himself the image and likeness of God; he is more like a beast than a man. Amen.

HOMILY 11

On Cheesefare Sunday

Do not lay up for yourselves treasures upon earth, where
moth and rust destroy and where thieves break in and steal;
but lay up for yourselves treasures in heaven, where neither
moth nor rust destroys and where thieves do not break in
and steal. For where your treasure is, there your heart will
be also. (Matt 6:19–21)

This is a saving commandment, directed to all of us,
from our Lord and Saviour Jesus Christ. Who has
never sinned against this commandment of our loving
Lord? Whose heart is not tied more or less to the earth,
to earthly treasures, whatever they may be? Who, for
example, is not attached to his flesh, to earthly honor and
glory, to earthly riches, to earthly beauty, to all kinds of
earthly pleasures, in general, to all that is earthly, sometimes to the point of forgetting God and His holy commandments and saving intentions toward us, forgetting
the heavenly nature of his soul, its image and likeness to

67

God, that it is destined for eternal life in God and with God, its deep fall and the need to raise it up through sincere, profound, and irrevocable repentance, its correction, purification, and sanctification through grace? Who is it whose treasure is God alone and His holy commandments, the holy virtues, and who despises and humbles his flesh with its passions and lusts as the temporary servant clinging to its mistress, the soul, and that only so much enjoys the attention and care of the soul as far as it serves its higher, spiritual goals? Who is it who does not possess different idols in his heart, set on this holy place that should always be the throne of the Almighty God?

Thus all of us, beloved in the Lord brothers and sisters, must admit to this, that we gather treasures on earth, in our temporary shelter, that must pass away and disappear, and where the moths and rust of self-love and the passions and sins destroy these treasures, as they are perishable and impure, and where thieves— the demons—and perhaps people, break in and steal the heart as well as its treasure. For example, if your treasure is money, or carnal pleasures, or impersonal people whom your bestial passions have made soulless and turned into objects of gross pleasure, as well as turning yourself into an immoral, soulless being; or is your treasure only earthly knowledge, art, industry, handcrafts? For how long will these treasures belong to you? Maybe not today or tomorrow, but soon enough your earthly edifice, your body, will collapse, and your treasure, together with your body, will leave you, and so what will remain for you, for your soul? Nothing. But your soul is eternal, and it will need in the age to come eternal treasures characteristic to it, such as hope in Christ and love of God and neighbor, mercy, humility, purity, rectitude, gentleness, and, generally, all works of virtue. Where do you keep them? Are you stocking up on spiritual oil? Are you stocking up on spiritual treasures? Well, you'd better stock up quickly, while there is still time. *Lay up for yourselves treasures in heaven, where neither moth nor rust doth destroys and where thieves do not break in and steal* (Matt 6:20); because, I add, there lies the kingdom of incorruption, the kingdom of truth, where the devil is not present. *For*, says the Lord, *where your treasure is, there your heart will be also* (Matt 6:21). That is a great truth that we often forget, and others forget it permanently: where our treasures are, there are also our hearts. And because our treasures are on earth, so also our hearts are on earth; they have clung to earthly treasures, pleasures, most of which are gross and impure, and therefore are no longer in heaven, with God or His holy commandments, His advice, His promises and consolation.

During the liturgy, the priest, before consecrating the heavenly mysteries, utters on behalf of the Church: *let us lift up our hearts*; that is, let us raise our hearts to God, let us break away from all that is earthly. But who is able to resolutely raise up his heart, even during these awesome and all-saving minutes, if our hearts and thoughts are so busy with earthly treasures and pleasures, cares, with the objects of our everyday passions? How often during these minutes do spiritual thieves break into our hearts and steal our attention, our faith, our love of God, and our devotion to the saving mystery, to this universal sacrifice of intercession, propitiation, and thanksgiving? Why is this so? It is because where our treasures are, there also are our hearts. It is because, going to church to attend the consecration of the heavenly mysteries, we did not prepare our souls to worthily stand in church, did not set aside all earthly worries and cares, did not cleanse our hearts from evil passions, did not leave every sin at the threshold of the temple; we forgot that, while standing in church, we must stand as if in heaven, because here lies the throne of God and the heavenly, awesome, and saving sacrifice; here the heavenly powers invisibly serve with us, and with them the Most-Holy Queen of heaven and earth, the Most-Holy Mother of God, and all the saints, which we silently commemorate on the liturgy, before and after the consecration of the Holy Gifts, because it is also for them that the Church offers to God the sacrifice of thanksgiving.

The days of fasting and repentance are approaching, in which we must acknowledge our sins, remember them, grieve for them, have contrition in our hearts, repent, and correct ourselves. How will our Lent be? How will our repentance be? If God, His holy will, His righteousness and eternal life together with its infinite blessedness are our treasures, then our Lent will be sincere, unfeigned, and our repentance will be sincere, ardent, resolute, consistent; for only such a repentance can give us back our priceless treasure, lost because of our sins—our Lord Jesus Christ and His grace. However, if our treasure, our idol, will as usual be our passionate flesh, the adulterous and sinful world, together with its charming, alluring, yet soon disappearing goods, then our Lent will not be sincere, or will simply not happen, and our repentance will be only superficial, and therefore insincere, irresolute, mediocre, barren, which may God forbid happens to any of us; for such a repentance is sinful insensitivity, ingratitude to God, Who gives the gift of infinite mercy to sinners for the sake of eternal life; it is a violation of the gifts of the Holy Spirit, Who cleanses our sins for the sake of the merits of Christ and Who sanctifies our souls and bodies.

Therefore, let all take heed to yourselves carefully, where your treasure is, on earth or in heaven! *For where your treasure is, there your heart will be also* (Matt 6:21).

On the Wednesday
of the First Week of Great Lent

Beloved, we have been fasting for four days and today is the fourth day in which we have attended divine services. Do our souls receive any benefit from fasting? This question each person should ask himself, and pay attention to his heart: are there any changes in it, has it stopped loving and committing sins? Moreover, it is necessary to realize: do the divine services have any effect on me, do I leave church with a pious mood, or do the services for me simply pass by as something foreign to me, so that I stand in church with cold indifference, I pray only out of habit, I perform prostrations without heartfelt compunction for my sins? Thus, beloved brethren, it is imperative for each person to realize this regarding the holy deed of the fast, whether it is being successful, or whether the work is being done in vain. We provide for ourselves an account of secular, often unimportant, matters; why not look with examining eyes also on this holy deed? Simply remember, beloved, for what you are preparing. You are preparing to approach the heavenly, most-pure, life-giving, awesome Mysteries of the Body and Blood of Jesus Christ, our God; you are preparing to be united with the Most-Pure God Himself! Ah! How after considering this can we not turn all our attention to this preparation?!

Therefore, beloved, let us look upon our preparation with strict eyes, and let us take care to exert all our efforts so that it will be to the benefit of our soul. How can we do this? The most important thing to do is this: let each one have his heart under control; the greatest attention must be paid to the heart, for in it lies all of man's malice; or better, the heart is itself the sinful, ungodly man, it is the working habitation of sin. Our hearts, beloved, have turned completely away from God, its Creator, and have turned completely toward the world and its illusions; in the heart are all our lusts, all our passions, all that is contrary to God. As you can see, it is necessary to effect a major change within oneself; from love of the world, its pleasures and sin, it is necessary to turn ourselves toward love of God, Whom we must love before and above everything else. This is no easy task, especially for those who so strongly love the world; moreover, *that friendship with the world*, according to the Apostle, *is enmity with God* (Jas 4:4). However, we will not fear that which is difficult: what is difficult and impossible for us is easy and possible for God: *with God all things are possible* (Matt 19:26). And so, the divine services will help you more than anything else in your holy deed of turning away from the world and toward God: simply stand and listen attentively to everything with a humble spirit, and holy thoughts and feelings will come to you without fail; it is impossible for the man who is vigilant and humble, who desires to unite himself to God, not to be visited by the spirit of compunction and contrition. Although there is much that you do not understand, yet you do understand some things, and it is true, there is also much that you do understand; therefore, these things that you do understand, absorb them in your heart, reflect on them; from listening to the holy words of the Church produce your own holy thoughts and feelings, and your preparation, with God's help, will be successful.

After all, our soul is not a land that is entirely barren for good. Can she be barren after she has been nourished with so much of God's grace that has rained upon her? Next, contemplate just how many of you perhaps are preparing yourselves for the last time, and that perhaps death will come all of a sudden and you will not be able to confess and commune of the Holy Mysteries before your death. In fact, *the ax is laid to the root of the trees*, the trees signify us, *therefore every tree which does not bear good fruit*, that is, people who do not perform good deeds, *is cut down and thrown into the fire* (Matt 3:10).

With what attention to oneself must each person prepare himself during this Lent in order to cleanse himself of his sins assuredly, perhaps for the last time. Furthermore, imagine more often how after your preparation and confession you will approach the Most-Pure Mysteries. However, if you approach them with uncorrected hearts, unworthily, then you commune to your own judgment and condemnation and *will be guilty of the body and blood of the Lord* (1 Cor 11:27), and after communion will be no better; on the contrary, you will have made yourselves even worse.

With such reflections fortify yourselves in your ascetic efforts of preparation, and pray in Church as sincerely as possible, with your whole hearts; say to the Lord, Who hearkens unto you as sincerely and as often as possible: *God, be merciful to me a sinner!* (Luke 18:13), God, cleanse me a sinner! Countless times have we sinned, O Lord, forgive us! Remember that only these words, *God, be merciful to me a sinner*, justified the publican. Why? Because they were spoken without any pretense, from the depths of the heart, from the perfect recognition of his guilt before God and the persistent determination to correct himself. And all of us, beloved, are such sinners that we have no excuses to make before God; we are not worthy to raise our eyes to heaven. How can we not say with all our souls: God, be merciful to us sinners! God, cleanse us sinners! Countless times have we sinned, Lord, forgive us! Amen.

HOMILY 13

On Repentance

If anyone sins, we have an Advocate with the Father, Jesus Christ the righteous. And He Himself is the propitiation for our sins. (1 John 2:1–2)

Today, beloved brethren, you will repent. I would like to instill in you, as it is my duty as a pastor, with what is expected of the person who comes to confession, so that his confession will be true, pleasing to God, and bring salvation to his soul. Namely, what is required of a repentant person is compunction for his sins, the intention to correct his life, faith in Christ, and hope in His mercy.

And so, first of all, it is required to feel compunction for your sins. However, this is something we as father confessors do not see in our spiritual children.

A great number of people come to confession with complete indifference in their souls, and, if they were not asked anything, they would either say nothing, or would speak very generally about how they "are sinful, spiritual father, having committed every sin." If only they said that in sincere recognition of their guilt, but no, what is worse, they say that without any conscience of their sins, and often they do it so that confession will be over quickly. Beloved! Let us not turn God's deed of extreme mercy toward us sinners into an occasion for God's wrath. Why are we so insensitive?! Have we nothing to regret during confession?! Not only are we sinful, but even if we spent our entire lives grieving over our sins, it would not be anything special, but only what we should in fact do. Ah! If one of us ever said that he is without sins, then he would be fooling himself, and finding the truth in him would be pointless.

Can you not see your sins? Pray to God, so that He will grant you to see them; it is not in vain that you have often repeated after the priest in Church: *Lord! Grant me to see my failings!* Let us at least now, through our common efforts, try to see our sins so that afterward during confession we will confess them with heartfelt compunction. And so, our first and most important sin is that we, being great sinners, do not feel that we are sinners, who are deserving not of God's mercy, but of His punishment! Let us first of all condemn ourselves for this insensitivity, and let us say to the Lord with our whole soul: Lord and Master of my life, I am an insensitive sinner, I am the greatest sinner, and I cannot feel my sins; this must be because my sins have multiplied more than the sands, and I am filled completely with sins, as an infirm person with smallpox. I repent before You, my Lord and God, of my insensitivity with all my heart, and I pray to You: Let me feel with all my heart how much I have angered, and continue to anger, You. Oh! This imaginary, pharisaical righteousness of ours, how much it has ruined and continues to ruin people! And to our ruin it strikes our heart especially during our time of preparation, during the very act of confession, and before the mystery of Holy Communion.

But let us look further, what sins have we committed against God most of all? If we are unbelieving people, if we live here on earth not for heaven, neither for God nor our salvation, but for the earth and its pleasures, namely, if we live for the flesh and its satisfaction, and not for our eternal soul, not for its future life, is this not a great sin? What happened? Did we forget about how our Lord Jesus Christ suffered for us, how He shed His Most-Pure Blood for us on the cross, and how he gloriously was resurrected?! Did He not do this for us in order to raise us to heaven? His coming to earth, His divine teachings, His miracles, His prophecies, for example, regarding the future, terrible judgment, the resurrection of the dead on the last day, the blessedness that awaits the righteous and the eternal torments that await sinners, were they not all for us? Finally, His suffering, His resurrection from the dead, and His ascension to heaven, were they not done for us?

Therefore, if it is true that we must live here on earth for the life of the age to come, then is it not a sin to live not for that life, but to live here on earth with all our heart and thoughts turned toward what is earthly? And how many sins originate from the fact that we want to live well on earth and do not believe wholeheartedly in the future, blessed life? How much malice, hatred, greed, envy, avarice, and deceit originate from this? From it originate all the vices, all carnal lusts, all the passions of the soul. Let us also repent of this, that is, let us repent of the fact that we lack faith, if we are not unbelievers altogether, and that we either do not live here for God and for the salvation of our souls, or live very little. Also let us repent that there is very little, if any, hope in our hearts for the future life. We also suffer from the great sin of ingratitude to God, of lack of love for Him for His countless, indescribable mercies. I think that this every person from time to time sees in himself.

Behold, all of you who are able to walk, all who are healthy physically and spiritually, gifted with intellect by God the Creator, with free will; what were you not so long ago? You were nothing; the Lord brought all of you from nonbeing into being, and since then He has given you everything: He gave you a soul with all its faculties, a body, with its wise and beautiful arrangement. He gave you and continues to give you food for the nourishment of your body, garments to clothe it. He gave you a corner of your own in His earth, and shelter, in your homes; He nourishes you with the invaluable, life-giving food of His Body and Blood, delighting you and comforting you with It; He gladdens you with the hearing of His word, He forgives your countless sins, He constantly protects your life, as a mother protects the life of her child; He gives us his future kingdom, and there is nothing He does not do out of His love for us, ungrateful sinners. It is impossible to number all of his blessings. And how do we repay His love for us, a love that knows no bounds or measure? We repay it with transgressions, with immorality, with ingratitude. Therefore, let us tearfully repent of our ingratitude before God, of our lack of love for Him, and also let us with tears ask Him to grant us the gift of love. *Bless the Lord, O my soul. And forget not all His benefits* (Ps 103:2).

The intention to correct his life is also required of the repentant person; pay attention to this. On your way to confession, tell yourself: after confession I will try with all my strength to correct my life from all the sins of which I wish to repent. I will deceive myself no more; I will not lie to God, nor will I insult again the mystery of repentance. Help me, Lord; strengthen the powers of my soul, Lord! What benefit is there from such a repentance after which, without any remorse, the person once again gives himself over to the same sins of which he repented? On such people the following proverb is fulfilled: *'A dog returns to his own vomit,'* and *'a sow, having washed, to her wallowing in the mire'* (2 Pet 2:22).

Finally, a repentant person also must have faith in Christ and hope in His mercy. Every person who approaches confession must believe that during the Mystery Christ Himself stands invisibly and receives his confession; he must believe that only Christ can forgive sins, as He, through His suffering, through His Most-Pure Blood, and through His death, obtained for Himself from the Heavenly Father the right to forgive us all our transgressions without insulting the divine justice, and that He, according to His mercy, is always ready to forgive our every sin, if only we confess them with heartfelt compunction and have the intention to be better from now on, and to have faith in Him in our hearts. *Your faith has made you well. Go in peace* (Mark 5:34). He speaks within each person who repents as he should, after receiving absolution from the priest.

Let us all repent with pure hearts; let us all take care to correct our lives; let us bring to God the fruits of repentance. Amen.

On the Communion
of the Holy Mysteries

Receive ye the Body of Christ, taste ye of the fountain of immortality. (Communion hymn)

In this chalice before you, O flock who bears the name of Christians, lie the divine Body and Blood of our Lord Jesus Christ, and you have prepared yourselves and confessed your sins in order to commune of these holy, immortal, and life-giving Mysteries. In order to receive them worthily, it is required of each and every one of us first to have the simple-hearted faith of children, that you receive, in the form of bread and wine, the most pure Body and Blood of the Saviour; that you receive the Saviour Himself in your lips and hearts, that you become one body and one blood with Him, one spirit, as it is said: *For we are members of His body, of His flesh and of His bones* (Eph 5:30); *he who eats My flesh and drinks My blood abides in Me, and I in him* (John 6:56); and *he who is joined to the Lord is one spirit with Him* (1 Cor 6:17); for in this particle of the Body and Blood of Christ-God that you receive, the whole Jesus Christ is to be found, as the soul is in the body.

Second, a perfect, unwavering hope in the Lord's mercy is required of you, that He, as heavenly fire, will consume and purify you of your sins through His blood; that is why each of us, acknowledging his unworthiness to receive the divine Mysteries, must give himself over completely to the Lord's mercy, in order that He Himself, through His grace, may make us worthy to receive the holy Mysteries. Let every person be of good hope, and let no one hesitate, or be fainthearted or depressed, imagining his own sinfulness and lewdness; everyone receives from the chalice the Master's mercy and great forgiveness, and the cleansing of sins. Simply have faith and hope.

Third, it is required that the communicants have a great, ardent, and angel-like love toward the Saviour; every one of us must respond to the Lord's love with love: for, tell me, how great is God's love toward us sinners, in that God Himself became incarnate for us, suffered, died and was resurrected, gave us as food and drink His own divine Body and Blood, and through this was united to us in the closest union possible, mixed with us, making us partakers of His divine nature! What mother or father has ever loved their children as the Lord has loved us? And for what purpose does the Lord unite with us through the holy Mysteries? In order to cleanse us from the defilement of sin, compared to which there is nothing more disgusting or terrible; in order to transmit to us His holiness, His divine life, peace, consolation, joy, lightness, sweetness, freedom, of which there is nothing more precious or desirable in the world; and once we are cleansed of our sins, transformed, and renewed, to take us with Himself into the heavens, to eternal life and blessedness: for no one can be in paradise with their sins and passions: *Whoever eats My flesh and drinks My blood has eternal life*, says the Lord, *and I will raise him up at the last day* (John 6:54).

Therefore, being able to commune with the divine Mysteries, ignite your hearts with love for the Saviour. O Holy Spirit, Consoler, Treasury of good things, pour Your love in our hearts!

Fourth, a change of heart is required of you. Until now, many of you have loved sin, all have either willingly or unwillingly indulged in sin; now let everyone make every effort to hate it; for sin is a product of the devil, it is opposition to God; let everyone try to change this in the depths of their soul. You desire to taste the Body and Blood of the divine Lamb, the meek and forgiving Lord Jesus Christ: be yourselves as meek and forgiving lambs, patient, obedient to the will of God, of the Church, of your parents, of your superiors, of the elderly. You receive the Body and Blood of the Saviour, and He is all love, and all evil and enmity are repugnant to Him: let us also try to live in mutual love; forgive each other's offenses, to not render evil for evil, or injury for injury. Approach the Lord, the Heavenly King, Who leads us all to heaven; try to contemplate on things on high, try to acquire heavenly customs; leave all passion for earthly things, which are corruptible and perishable, which enslave and ruin the soul; love your heavenly fatherland, the heavenly city of Jerusalem, where the Mother of God and the saints abide, and where all of us must strive to go. Leave all impurities and sinful passions; let everyone show that he has changed for the better, let everyone show improvement; let everyone bring any good fruit of good works to the Master; let everyone bring forth worthy fruits of repentance! O Lord! Transform us, renew us Yourself!

Finally, in order that we may preserve these heavenly gifts, the most pure Body and Blood of Christ, in fifth place it is required that we pay attention to ourselves, to our thoughts, our hearts, to all its feelings and inclinations, curbing its sinful desires and aspirations. We must also abstain from food and drink, we must abstain from idle talk, foul language, oaths, and all lies; in a word, you must protect yourself from all that is contrary to Christ, the Saviour of our souls. Remember that through communion the Lord deifies you, makes you divine; try to live in a divine way, in all holiness, truth, and justice. You are children of Christ and God: what type of life befits the children of God?

May the Lord grant all of you to worthily and fruitfully receive the divine Mysteries. *For he who eats and drinks* the divine Body and Blood *in an unworthy manner eats and drinks judgment to himself* (1 Cor 11:29), says the Apostle Paul. Therefore, let us approach with faith and love, so that we may be partakers of eternal life. Amen.

HOMILY 15

On the First Sunday of Great Lent, the Sunday of Orthodoxy

Hereafter you shall see heaven open. (John 1:51)

I congratulate many of you, as well as myself, beloved brothers and sisters, with the indescribable mercy of God, with spiritual renewal, obtained through the ascetic efforts of preparation, prayer, fasting, and repentance, and especially through the communion of the most-pure and life-giving Mysteries of the Body and Blood of the Lord. And during this brief time we have already been able to know within ourselves the benefits of fasting and prayer, not to mention the benefits of preparing ourselves, of confession and communion. If, naturally, we sincerely made use of this time for our salvation and sincerely fulfilled the conditions of the fast and preparation; if we abstained from excess in food and drink, prayed sincerely, humbled ourselves before God and our neighbors, were merciful, recognized the multitude of our faults and transgressions and firmly repented of them, having a firm intention of not committing them again, and finally, sincerely confessed them and received absolution and remission of sins, we were granted to taste of the life-giving Food. But did all of us really benefit from the week that went by? Did our hearts become closer to God, to the Most-Pure Mother of Life, to the Church, to our Holy Guardian Angel, and to the saints of God? Have we sincerely loved truth and virtue, and have we hated all falsehood and iniquity? Do we sincerely love God and neighbor; do we feel a greater spiritual affinity with each other, as members of the One Body of Christ, as members of Christ? *For we, though many, are one bread* of the sacrament, *and one body, for we all partake of that one bread* (1 Cor 10:17).

Do we feel with our hearts how the streams of transgressions do not flow with such impudence and violence toward our souls as they did before our preparation and communion, and have noticeably dried within us, and we have become purer, freer, calmer, passionless, better, with softer hearts, more inclined to everything that is good and beneficial? Has the hunger for carnal pleasures and greed diminished within us? Have we become meeker, more patient, more compassionate toward our neighbors? Do we look more often to the heavens, to our true and eternal homeland, and do we look more passionlessly upon all that is earthly, as being temporary, transient, and passing? For see how many people among us were taken by death in a short time, and how death constantly carries its victims. If this is so, if we have become better and more reasonable, then once again I congratulate you and myself with God's great mercy, and together with you I pray that the Lord will establish this good attitude and disposition of heart in myself and in you. But let none of us be tempted by that evil thought that now, thank God, we have cast off from ourselves the burden of sin and can go back to living the way we used to live, and sin the way we used to sin because, we would say, who is without sin?! It is true, brothers and sisters, that no one is without sin; however, to live like once we lived, and sin like we used to, after being renewed through repentance and communion is not proper, is not becoming, should not be done by any Christian.

The Holy Church, through the father confessor, gives the following admonition to every repentant sinner: "In all these points thou must henceforth be upon thy guard. For thou hast received a second Baptism, according to the Christian Mystery. And thou must see to it that, God helping, thou make a good beginning. But, above all, thou must not bear thyself lightly toward these things, lest thou become a cause of scorn to men; for these things do not befit a Christian. But may God, by his grace, aid thee to live honorably, uprightly and devoutly." This is how the Church exhorts the repentant. And common sense also exhorts us, for which person, after having cleansed himself, desires to once again deliberately defile himself? Only pigs, after being washed, go back to wallowing in the mire; only a dog tends to turn again to his own vomit (2 Pet2:22). *See, you have been made well. Sin no more, lest a worse thing come upon you* (John 5:14), said the Lord to the paralytic who was healed. And something much worse can happen also to us if we neglect virtue after repentance; then the grace of God will abandon us due to our carelessness and negligence toward ourselves. Repentance and communion open for us the heavens and the kingdom of heaven, for, as the Lord says, *Whoever eats My Flesh and drinks My Blood has eternal life ... and abides in Me, and I in him* (John 6:54, 56).

How can we not cherish the gift received: eternal life and Christ dwelling in us, and us in Him! The heavens are opened to us through repentance and communion as it is written: *hereafter you shall see heaven open* (John 1:51). What wonderful mercy! Through our sins the heavens were closed, as the strongest keeps and castles, but through repentance they were opened; let us make use of this mercy of God before they close again for us. For only God knows whether they will once again open for us after we have closed them again through our voluntary sins. For many people they will close forever. The foolish virgins knocked on the closed doors, saying: '*Lord! Lord! Open to us,*' and they were told: '*Assuredly, I say to you, I do not know you';* and to all of us it was said: *Watch therefore, for you know neither the day nor the hour in which the Son of man is coming* (Matt 25:11–13). Amen.

On the Sunday of Orthodoxy

Behold, an Israelite indeed, in whom is no deceit! (John 1:47)

Our Lord Jesus Christ spoke such words about one Israelite, Nathanael, who lived in the city of Cana of Galilee, when he went to meet Jesus Christ by the suggestion of his friend Philip, in order to ascertain whether Jesus Christ really was the Messiah promised to Israel. *Philip found Nathanael, and said to him, 'We have found Him, of whom Moses in the law, and also the prophets, wrote—Jesus of Nazareth, the son of Joseph.' And Nathanael said to him, 'Can anything good come out of Nazareth?' Philip said to him, 'Come and see.' Jesus saw Nathanael coming toward Him, and said of him, 'Behold, an Israelite indeed, in whom is no deceit!' Nathanael said to him, 'How do you know me?' Jesus answered and said unto him, 'Before Philip called you, when you were under the fig tree, I saw you'* (John 1:45–48). That is, saw all your thoughts, your faith, your hope for the Messiah, and your future service. The Lord, Who sees our hearts, clearly touched the liveliest chords of Nathanael's heart, his most intimate thoughts, his most intimate desires and hopes, showing him firsthand His divine omniscience, and thus Nathanael was caught in the faith of Christ. He shouted: *Rabbi! You are the Son of God! You are the King of Israel!* (John 1:49). Afterward Nathanael became His disciple under the name Bartholomew, that is, one of the twelve.

But why on this Sunday, which is called the Sunday of Orthodoxy, did the Church appoint the reading of this Gospel passage about the conversation between the Lord and Nathanael? Because, in the words of the Lord, Nathanael displayed the nature of a true, or Orthodox, Christian, and in general the nature of the true Orthodox Church of Christ. *Behold, an Israelite indeed*, said the Lord about Nathanael, *in whom is no deceit;* that is, behold a man who thinks, reasons, believes, hopes, speaks, and acts correctly, frankly, and firmly, just as Nathanael immediately and correctly believed in Jesus Christ as the Son of God, and never again wavered in his faith and hope, did not change his mind regarding His divine Person. Is this not also how a true Christian must be? Is this not how the entire divinely established society of Orthodox Christians must be? Is it not how the Orthodox Church must, as it is, be? What high praise Nathanael received from Him, who tries all hearts and reigns, in the words: *Behold, an Israelite indeed, in whom is no deceit!* What high praise for the Christian of whom the Lord says: behold a true Christian, in whom is no deceit; as well as for the Church of which the Lord says: behold a Church, in which there is neither deceit nor the vain inventions of men; that is, a Church that is true in all its teachings, mysteries, divine services, government, and throughout all of its structure.

And these are precisely how all of our saints are, how our entire Orthodox Church is, since its beginning until our days, as evidenced by the objective history of the Church and by God Himself, through the various signs and miracles performed in the Church. It is, according to the Apostle, *the pillar and ground of the truth* (1 Tim 3:15); *a glorious church, not having spot or wrinkle or any such thing* (Eph 5:27). And with what sanguinary feats, what struggles with the enemies of truth, with how many deaths of those who were zealous for the purity, sanctity, and orthodoxy of the faith and the Church, my brethren, was the orthodoxy of our faith acquired for all of us, our guide toward eternal life! Just as rivers of blood were shed for the preservation and integrity of our nation, and in it our Orthodox faith, by our ancestors, Russian soldiers and leaders, who fought against pagans, Muslims, and other Christians who were strangers to the Orthodox Church, so were rivers of blood also shed for the preservation of the Orthodox faith by apostles, prophets, and martyrs; much suffering was endured by reverend fathers and other champions of the faith.

And what about us, children of the Orthodox Church? Do we preserve this most precious heritage, the Orthodox Faith? Do we follow its teachings, commandments, rules, statutes, advice? Do we love to offer this service to God, *the fruit of our lips, giving thanks to His name* (Heb 13:15)? Are we renewed by it? Do we sanctify ourselves every day, do we correct ourselves, do we attain the perfection the saints attained? Do we perfect ourselves in our love for God and neighbor, do we cherish our faith, do we consider it the greatest mercy of God, the very first and greatest benefit of life the fact that we are fortunate to belong to the Orthodox Church, which is the One, Holy, Catholic and Apostolic Church?

What is our answer to these questions, if we desire to answer honestly? To our shame we must confess that many, many Orthodox Christians not only do not have the Orthodox faith in their hearts and lives, but also do not have it even in their tongues, and faith has either completely disappeared from their lives or they have become completely indifferent toward any faith: Catholicism, Lutheranism, Judaism, Islam, even paganism. We hear from many people that you can please God in every faith, that is, as if every faith is pleasing to God, and as if God is indifferent to truth and falsehood, right and wrong. Look at the consequences of ignoring one's faith, of the ignorance of the spirit and history of their Church, alienation from its life and divine services, the consequences of ignoring concepts of Orthodoxy, Heterodoxy, and other faiths!

There is an episode from news that somewhere in Russia, during a test, a teacher said that the event of the offering of Isaac as sacrifice was nonsensical. This is darkness, chaos, ruinous ignorance! A Christian, as a member of the Church, must know his faith and try to live according to it, be saved by his faith, because the enemies of our salvation do not sleep, and seek our destruction at every hour; a Christian must not abandon his faith, as being simply a specialty belonging to a mere few, or like an unnecessary toy, appropriate only for childhood, or as something worthy only of the uneducated masses. Those who suffer from such delusions would do well to remember the venerable antiquity of our faith, the beginning of the modern human race and its direct origin from God, and that in our faith were saved people of all kinds, ranks, genders: glorious kings, wise philosophers, legislators and great orators, noble and simple folk, rich and poor, male and female, the beauty and glory of mankind.

We must also mention, for the glory of the Orthodox faith, that no other religion except Orthodoxy can bring man to moral perfection or holiness and perfect agreeableness to God, as evidenced by the history of the Church and the incorrupt and wonderworking remains of the holy saints of God, and by the wonderful feats of the saints of the Orthodox Church, through which they were perfectly pleasing to God, and who even while they were still alive were clairvoyant and wonderworkers. And so it should be, according to common sense: only the perfect faith can bring one to perfection, with all divine powers, all the spiritual armor of God against the passions of the flesh, the world, and the devil.

If nowadays many Orthodox Christians live worse than Muslims and pagans, so much so that the head of all Muslims in Russia publicly proclaimed in St Petersburg praise for his fellow Muslims for the fact that among them there are no people so wicked as among the Christians, who attempted to end the life of the tsar. This truly impious life of the Christians must not in the least, of course, be blamed on the Orthodox Faith, which is unwavering in its principles of truth and holiness, according to the promise of the Saviour Himself and the testimony of history. Such people, even though they came from us, were never one of us in essence, but only in name.

Yes, my brethren, only the Orthodox Faith purifies and sanctifies human nature stained by sin; it renews the corrupted, especially through the mysteries of baptism, repentance, and communion. It illumines those who are darkened, heals those who are wounded by sins, warms those who are cold, and through the grace of the Holy Spirit makes fragrant those who reek of the passions. It quickens those who are dying, reunites to God those who had turned away from Him, returns to Him those who were alienated from Him. It strengthen the weak, beautifies and adorns the disfigured, raises the fallen, frees those who are captive, fills with love those who are hostile, as it did with the Apostle Paul and many others. It fills blasphemers with incessant glorification of God, fills those who are despairing with hope, consoles those who are sad, delivers those who are guilty from condemnation and punishment in Gehenna. It pacifies those who are confused, strengthens the faint, frees the oppressed, enriches the unrighteous with righteousness, turns the cunning honest, evil into good, corrects the depraved, makes the greedy abstentious, the adulterous chaste, the avaricious generous. It gives wisdom to the foolish, makes heavenly those who are earthly, refines those who are rough, makes spiritual those who are carnal. Turns lovers of things into lovers of God, lovers of self into self-denying lovers of all, those who are demon-like into god-like, and, what miracle, makes them divine! Behold the miracles the Orthodox Faith works in man!

Would you like to be convinced of this? Read the lives of the saints, the history of the Church, and you will see firsthand all of these miracles in the lives of the saints. You will see wolves turning into lambs, fornicators and harlots turning into righteous and angelic people, lovers of money turning into merciful people, hedonists becoming abstinent; you will see people of earthly power, grandeur, and luxury in the humble garbs of monastics. How authentic the true Christians were; they were angels in the flesh, citizens of heaven here on earth, and at the same time, faithful servants of their earthly homeland, like the Forty Martyrs of Sebaste who we also commemorate today! See what our Orthodox Faith can do for those people who sincerely observe it and follow its guidance! Why does it not also effect such saving changes within us? Because of our lack of faith, or unbelief, because of our frivolity, corruption, and the impenitence in our hearts; because of the passions that grow stronger within us and have complete control over us, because of our falling away from the Church, and because many of us do not in the least instill within ourselves the spirit of the Church, and many others insincerely, weakly, and only slightly more formally belong to it. Because of this, all the modern social vices arose in us: murder, suicide, regicide, arson, theft of public property, exorbitant luxury, debauchery, extravagance, and the pursuit of all sorts of sensual pleasures.

For us to be true Orthodox Christians, we must first of all have a living, constant communion with the Orthodox

Church: that is, we must partake in its prayers, teachings, and mysteries; we must diligently study our faith and be instilled with and live in its spirit; we must be guided by its rules, commandments, statutes, and more important, we must restore within ourselves the image of true and deep repentance of a true Orthodox Christian according to the image of the saints, old and new, or better, according to the image of our Lord Jesus Christ Himself, Who said: *For I have given you an example, that you should do as I have done to you* (John 13:15), so that the Lord may say of us, as once he said of Nathanael: *Behold, an Israelite indeed, in whom is no deceit* (John 1:47). Amen.

On the Second Sunday
of Great Lent

Son, your sins are forgiven you. (Mark 2:5)

The paralytic was evidently brought to Christ to be healed from the illness of paralysis, which kept him confined to a bed. However, Christ first heals his soul from its sins, and only then heals his body from the illness. *Son*, He says to the paralytic, *your sins are forgiven you*, and after forgiving his sins, He said: *Arise, take up your bed, and go to your house* (Mark 2:11). What does this way of healing mean? It means that the illnesses that befall us are the consequences of our sins, and that it is impossible to be completely free from illnesses unless we first cleanse ourselves from our sins, just as it is impossible to destroy the consequences without first destroying its causes. And just as in our days it is common to have many infirm people, who are looking for means to be healed from their infirmities, let us now talk about the close connection that exists between our sins and our bodily afflictions.

Is it really true that there is such a close connection between our sins and our bodily sicknesses and suffering, that the infirmities of the body, more or less strong and long-lasting, are in fact the consequences of our sins? Such a connection between sins and infirmities truly does exist: sins are destructive to the soul as well as the body. The holy apostle speaks of sin thusly: *the wages of sin is death* (Rom 6:23): that is, sin, as a cruel tyrant, collects tribute from the people who work for him; and all people work for him. This tribute is death. Therefore, death is the necessary tribute for our sins, and death is almost always preceded by diseases that are more or less prolonged. From this it is clear that a close connection exists between sins and infirmities. When there will be no more sin, then also there will be no more disease and death. That is why in the age to come there are no diseases. *There shall be no more death, nor sorrow, nor crying. There shall be no more pain* (Rev 21:4), testifies St John the Evangelist through divine revelation.

Often due to our sins God Himself will directly send a disease, for example, *to deliver such a one unto Satan for the destruction of the flesh* (1 Cor 5:5), as it happened to the man who had his father's wife, as mentioned by the Apostle Paul in his epistle to the Corinthians; or He deprives one of the use of the senses and members of the body, or subjects others to various diseases. In this case, illnesses are the works of the Lord's goodness, Who has *no pleasure in the death of the wicked, but that the wicked turn from his way and live* (Ezek 33:11). People are extremely tempted by the sweetness of sin and die, but God, according to His goodness, does not want our eternal destruction, but wants to make all of us partakers of His blessedness. However, how can He do this when man doesn't want to pay any attention to either future bliss or eternal torment, and when he gives himself over completely to earthly pleasures and entertainment? While he is still alive, man feels within himself the fullness of his strength and thinks how convenient it is to live here as he pleases. How do we compel him to think about God, about eternal life for which he was created, or compel him to have recourse to faith and the virtues so that they become the life of his heart? The best means for this, in this case, are illnesses and suffering. One has only to look at a sick person or someone subject to some other sort of misfortune to be convinced of how beneficial illnesses and misfortunes can sometimes be. When this happens, man begins to think about when he will meet God, he enters within himself and sees just how insignificant and fleeting he is: *All flesh is grass. And all its loveliness is like the flower of the field* (Isa 40:6). He sees that all that is earthly is dust and vanity, and that only God and the virtues are eternal, that man needs to serve God in this life in spirit and in truth, and to stock up on good deeds for eternal life.

Brethren! All of us become ill or are beset by some misfortune, and we all wish, according to the law of self-preservation, to be healthy and well. Let us remember that our illnesses, which often are the fruits of our transgressions, of our own negligence or unrestrained life since the beginning, very often, according to their strength and duration, are God's punishment for our sins. If we wish to be free from illness, we ought first to destroy their internal cause, our sins; then the external misfortunes will go away of themselves. Let us remember that infirmities and death would not be in the human race if sin had not entered into the world through the first man. Let others imagine whatever they want to be the causes for diseases; however, if they delve deeply into the essence of the matter, they will arrive at the same explanation for what the main causes are. At some point man's physical nature was severely damaged, and is now damaged, by some internal, hostile force, and because of this it is sensitive to the slightest natural change, which is the reason it has become so weak and easily destructible.

Now is the time for spiritual healing. Let us flee from sin, from which our souls so painfully suffer, and our *healing shall spring forth speedily* (Isa 58:8). Amen.

HOMILY 18

On the Second Sunday
of Great Lent

And again He entered Capernaum after some days, and it was heard that He was in the house. Immediately many gathered together, so that there was no longer room to receive them, not even near the door. And He preached the word to them. Then they came to Him, bringing a paralytic who was carried by four men. (Mark 2:1–3)

I f an earthly king, or the son of the king, visits a city or a village and stays at one of its houses, a great number of people will gather near the house because all want to see his clear kingly eyes, carefully turned toward the entire realm and toward all its subjects, and all want to listen to the king's gracious speech. The dignity of a king is so lofty, so important is his service to God and the people here on earth, that all feel toward him a peculiar involuntary reverence, and often a simple look from him is enough to enthrall someone. However, there was a time when the Heavenly King Himself, the King of all the world, the unoriginate God, the Creator of heaven and earth, the King of all earthly kings appeared on earth and lived among men, wandering from city to city, from one village to the next. What joy, what bliss it was to see the Heavenly King Himself; those most lucent, vigilant eyes looking at the entire universe; that gaze, which brings joy to angels and strikes fear in demons, and to hear, from his most sweet lips, a word that grants life, rest, joy, comfort to every sincere, upright soul! You may be jealous of those fortunate people who lived during the stay of Jesus Christ on earth. Don't be.

He is also with us now continually through His Divinity, His grace, His life-giving Mysteries, His divine Body and Most-Pure Blood; in this respect we are in no way resentful of the contemporaries of Jesus Christ, for we were not deprived of anything; in fact, we have received more than they have, because they did not have the bliss to taste His life-giving Body and Blood, whereas we taste them and become deified. The liturgy, during which this mystery is performed, illustrates for us the entire life of Jesus Christ, from His cradle to His ascension to heaven, and the holy Mysteries display His personal presence, the boundless love of the Lord for His rational creation; and the lofty manifestation of God in the flesh and in the form of a man show, my brethren, the dignity of the human nature, created according to God's image, but humiliated, disfigured, paralyzed, and mortified by sin. It assures us that if man will live in a righteous and holy manner, then he will be equal to the angels, and will live and rejoice with them for all eternity. It assures us that for God, after the Mother of God and the holy angels, there is no one dearer or more elevated than man, whose form He took, for whom He suffered, died, and rose again. It assures us that all of the heavens and the kingdom of heaven are man's inheritance, and that beside him there are no other heirs to whom was said: *Come, you blessed of My Father, inherit the kingdom prepared for you from the foundation of the world* (Matt 25:34).

But let us return to what was said in the Gospel. Jesus, it is said, *entered Capernaum after some days, and it was heard that He was in the house. Immediately many gathered together, so that there was no longer room to receive them, not even at the door* (Mark 2:1–2). The Hebrew city of Capernaum was located by the lake of Gennesaret, not far from the confluence of the river Jordan, and was one of the most flowering and populous cities of Galilee during the time of Jesus Christ. During the three-year period of His social ministry for the salvation of mankind, the Lord repeatedly stayed in Capernaum, preached in the Jewish synagogues, and worked many miracles. Among these, it was here that the paralytic who could not walk was healed, about whom we read in today's Gospel.

Here were also healed the servant of the Roman centurion, the mother-in-law of the Apostle Peter with many others, the woman with an issue of blood, two blind men, a man who was possessed, and it was in Capernaum that the daughter of Jairus, the leader of the synagogue, was resurrected. You could say that the inhabitants of this city in which Jesus Christ often stayed were happy, even overjoyed. However, I would not agree with you.

I could not say that the citizens of Capernaum were happy simply because the Son of God was often among them; I cannot say this because the citizens of Capernaum, having seen many times His miracles, His good deeds toward His fellow citizens, remained ungrateful before their Benefactor and Wonderwoker, they remained unbelievers, unrepentant sinners. The Lord Himself denounced this city, saying: *and you, Capernaum, who are exalted to heaven, will be brought down to Hades; for if the mighty works*, that is, the miracles, *which were done in you had been done in Sodom, it would have remained until this day*, that is, it would have repented. *But I say to you that it shall be more tolerable for the land of Sodom in the day of judgment than for you* (Matt 11:23–24). Now you can see why the citizens of Capernaum were unfortunate people, because even though they often saw the miracles of the Lord and heard His teachings, they remained unrepentant sinners and were condemned to hell.

My brethren! Let us consider ourselves: were we shown less favor from the Lord than the citizens of Capernaum? We are born by baptism through water and the Holy Spirit and are adopted by God; we are sanctified by the Holy Spirit through chrismation, and through communion we taste the very same Most-Pure Body and Blood of the Lord; through confession we are granted forgiveness of our sins after sincere repentance; through ordination we receive the constant teachers of the faith and Christian life, who perform the saving mysteries and guide us to God and eternal life; through holy unction we receive healing of our physical ailments by repenting of our sins. And what do we give the Lord for all His mercy toward us, all His miracles and His long-suffering toward us? Ingratitude, immorality, hardness of heart, unbelief, absent-mindedness, sinfulness, and impenitence. However, will it always be like this? Will the measure of the Lord's patience for us not soon be met? Is the Lord's sword not already hanging over our heads? Isn't the ax of death already laid at the root of the tree, at our hearts? Has hell not yet already opened its mouth to swallow us? Let us awaken, let us come to our senses, let us repent with our whole hearts while we still have time for repentance. Let us study the Word of God, diligently visit God's temple, and engage in philanthropy and charity. It is true, during Great Lent our churches sometimes are full of worshippers, like that house in which Jesus Christ was, so much so that the people barely fit in it. Glory be to God! If only the churches were filled with Christians more often! Yet the theater is filled much more often than our churches.

But let us continue with the explanation of the Gospel. *And He preached the word to them* (Mark 2:2). Everywhere He went the Lord preached the word, and this word was sweeter than honey from the honeycomb; it healed souls and bodies, it bent and transformed hearts, as it did with Saul; it raised the dead, cast out demons, threw the audacious to the ground, and commanded the elements, which obeyed the voice of the Almighty; it transformed the creation in a single moment; today this word is heard in the temple. Why are there so few who hear it and who obey it? Because of our absentmindedness, our love for the world, for its vain goods and pleasures. *You cannot*, said the Lord once and for all, *serve God and mammon* (Matt 6:24), that is, the world. But remember: this world will judge us on the last day. *Therefore we must give the more earnest heed to the things we have heard, lest we drift away* (Heb 2:1) internally from God. This is why the Holy Church requires our attention when the Gospel is read.

Then they came to Him, bringing a paralytic who was carried by four men. And when they could not come near Him because of the crowd, they uncovered the roof where He was. So when they had broken through, they let down the bed on which the paralytic was lying (Mark 2:3–4). How miserable is the man who, being fully conscious, cannot walk due to extreme weakness and must always rely on the help of others: he is a burden to himself and to others. Such a man was the paralytic mentioned in today's Gospel, and there are also such people among us, who are bound by paralysis and other afflictions. But there is a spiritual paralysis that is caused by sins, by passions, which is incomparably more dangerous and much more deserving of pity than physical paralysis because it often brings about eternal death.

In this respect every sinner is a paralytic. Every sin is accompanied by spiritual paralysis, as a consequence of falling away from God, in Whom is our life and our strength; it is as a fall unto death. And as we all sin, we are all paralytics. How can we be healed from this paralysis, from this foreshadowing of eternal death? Through sincere, profound, complete repentance of sins. That is why, of course, today's Gospel reading about the paralytic is appointed, so that his situation, which was a consequence of his sins, would touch our hearts and also dispose us to diligent repentance. That is why Jesus Christ healed the paralytic by first granting him forgiveness of his sins. *When Jesus saw their faith, He said to the paralytic, 'Son, your sins are forgiven you'* (Mark 2:5). From this it is clear that the paralytic was suffering as a result of his sins.

My brethren! Whenever you are sick, before doing anything else, offer God repentance for your sins, have recourse to the Almighty Healer, taste of His life-giving Body and Blood. There is a secret and intimate connection between sin and infirmity. *And some of the scribes were sitting there and reasoning in their hearts. 'Why does this Man speak blasphemies like this? Who can forgive sins but God alone?'* (Mark 2:6–7). To the sly, envious, and ambitious scribes, that is, to the learned Hebrew teachers, Jesus Christ's good deed seemed like blasphemy and scandalized them. The same happens today brethren: an evil person reduces good deeds to scandalous ones. You go to church to pray to God, you read sacred books, you withdraw from distractions, entertainment, spectacles, from the company of others, and they say, "behold a prude." You give alms and they say, "he is multiplying parasites." Would it not be better for these evil people to look at themselves, how they are, than to judge and condemn others? They must remember the words of the righteous Judge: *Judge not, that you be not judged* (Matt 7:1). Jesus Christ, Who knows the hearts of men, denounced the evil thoughts of His opponents by telling them: *Why do you reason about these things in your hearts? Which is easier, to say to the paralytic, 'Your sins are forgiven you,' or to say, 'Arise, take up your bed and walk'?* (Mark 2:8–9).

In fact, is it not equally impossible for a simple man to forgive another man just like himself the sins he committed against God, and to heal an illness with his word? Needless to say, it is impossible. For whom is this possible? Only for God; consequently, if Jesus Christ's word was deed—that is, if it eradicated sins, healed every illness, just as all these people saw it, including the scribes—then how could they accuse the Lord of blasphemy? If we look at this event with simplicity, then they should have believed that Jesus Christ is God because He forgives sins and heals illness by His word; however, they said, *He speaks blasphemies*. What did the Lord answer them? *'But that you may know that the Son of Man has power on earth to forgive sins'*—He said to the paralytic. *'I say to you, arise, and take up your bed, and go to your house.' Immediately he arose, took up the bed, and went out in the presence of them all, so that all were amazed and glorified God, saying, 'We never saw anything like this'* (Mark 2:10–12).

Do you see how His word became deed? The sins were forgiven, the paralysis went away, the man regained his full health and his strength; and both the forgiveness of sins and the healing of the infirmity showed that Jesus Christ is the Judge, the Giver of Life and God, and not a blasphemer as the scribes thought. My brethren! The power to forgive people their sins belongs to God alone, as Creator and Legislator; and who among you has not experienced within himself how Jesus Christ forgives and absolves us of every sin? How light, peaceful, and joyous our souls become when we repent of our sins with our whole hearts before the Lord and we hear the words of forgiveness: *son, you sins are forgiven you*. How joyous our soul becomes when we taste, with faith and love, of His divine Food, His Most-Pure Body and Blood! How also now those who are sick often recover their health soon after they repent of their sins before the priest and commune of Christ's Holy Mysteries! All of us have experienced countless times that Jesus Christ is our Judge, our Saviour, our Legislator, and our God; let us always diligently have recourse to Him with faith, so that we may receive from Him the usual, proven mercy of forgiveness of sins and spiritual peace together with physical health.

The treasure of mercy is always open to all: let everyone draw from it a thousand times a day; our countless sins will not be victorious over the infinite mercy of the Master, if only we, sinners, sincerely repent. May Your mercy be glorified, Lord, unto the ages of ages! And let us, brothers and sisters, be merciful to our neighbors. Once again I appeal to your charity with a petition for alms to those poor people unto which our parish ministers. Kindly do this in the name of God: *He who gives to the poor will not lack* (Prov 28:27). Amen.

On the Second Sunday of Great Lent

When Jesus saw their faith, He said to the paralytic, 'Son, your sins are forgiven you.' (Mark 2:5)

Once when our Lord and Saviour Jesus Christ was traveling through cities and villages preaching the kingdom of heaven, he went into the home of one of the citizens of Capernaum, and, as usual, he preached there. Many people gathered to listen to Him, so much so that it was impossible to even reach the doors of the house. Four men brought to this house a man who lived on a bed, sick with paralysis, so that he would be seen by Him Who healed *every sickness and every disease among the people* (Matt 9:35). But as it was impossible to make way through the crowd and approach Christ, they got up on the roof of the house, dismantled the tiled roof and, making an opening big enough to let down the paralytic, they lowered him down on his bed onto the floor at the very feet of the Lord. The Lord, seeing their faith, told the paralytic: *son, your sins are forgiven you*, and then, to show the unbelieving scribes through a clear miracle that He is the God-Man, possessing the power on earth to forgive sins, He told him: *I say to you, arise, take up your bed, and go to your house. Immediately he arose, took up the bed, and went out in the presence of them all* (Mark 2:11–12). Witnessing this miracle, all of the people were amazed and glorified God, testifying that they had never seen anything like it. Such was the reward from the God-Man for the faith of those who brought the paralytic!

Had this paralytic been brought to an earthly doctor, then he would undoubtedly have considered it superfluous to pay any attention to the paralytic's sins, but would have started to treat him from his physical paralysis using material means instead of spiritual ones. However, the Divine Wonderworker works differently: He heals the physical paralysis through the forgiveness of sins: *son, your sins are forgiven you*. Why is that? Because, certainly, spiritual paralysis, that is, his sins, were the cause for the physical paralysis. And, indeed, all illnesses and death originate from the sinful paralysis of the human soul. And for many thousands of years sin has generated all of the sicknesses of soul and body.

But for what reason did the Holy Church establish the gospel reading about the paralytic on this day? Certainly because it sees all of us as infirm paralytics, suffering from spiritual paralysis, caused by sin, and desires that all of us have recourse to Jesus Christ for healing. And indeed, we are all paralytics. Any sin we have in us is a paralysis. And each person can see in himself how sin is indeed spiritual paralysis. Our hearts become paralyzed from any form of sin, our minds are clouded for anything spiritual, our wills become weak to perform good, all of the foundations of our life become paralyzed, so to speak, because when our heart, the main engine of our lives, becomes paralyzed, then the whole man becomes paralyzed. That is why the Holy Church, knowing just how important firmness of heart and being immovable in the rock of faith and the commandments of God is, sings aloud to us: *Establish, O Lord, my wavering heart on the rock of Thy commandments* (Irmos of the Canon of St Andrew of Crete, Ode 3).

And thus, all of us are paralytics. Although some of us, when aroused by our consciences, become aware of our infirmity and move toward Christ to be treated for our sinful paralysis, others, alas, need the diligent help of others to sincerely recognize their infirmity and desire with their whole heart to receive healing from Jesus Christ. Ah! Who could, through the strength of their faith and a heartfelt counsel, be able to move these people, like the paralytic, to contrition of heart before the face of our Lord Jesus Christ, Who took upon Himself our sins and infirmities? Such a person would be rendering others the greatest Christian service. And there are many among us who are spiritual paralytics, who truly need the sincere help of others. They are so weak in faith, their hearts have become paralyzed by passions to such an extent, that on their own they are incapable of taking a single step in their faith and Christian life.

What then? Is it really possible that there is none among you, beloved, who could help your infirm brethren, who are weak in the faith? Is it really possible that among you there are no sincere believers who could help unbelievers with your living faith? Is it really possible that among you there are none who could instruct your brother who is ignorant, or who lives a dissolute life, and counsel him to turn to Christ with pure, heartfelt repentance? Answer me, brethren, if you were the ones weak in faith, or who led licentious, dissolute lives, would you not wish to be delivered from your pitiful spiritual paralysis, which has as its end the eternal torments in the fires of Gehenna? Do you wish to fall before Jesus Christ Himself and be healed by Him? This is very convenient. Jesus Christ is present in this holy temple every Friday, and if necessary on other days as well, and receives all those who are paralyzed by sin, and according to their faith, heals them through the priest. Every time when a sinner repents sincerely of his sins, the Lord Himself tells him inwardly: *son, your sins are forgiven you.* What, then, prevents you from approaching Jesus Christ with faith to be healed by Him? Come, be healed; all are welcome to come now and throughout Great Lent. Christ Himself receives each and every one. The priests are simply witnesses who stand before Him, mediators between Him and you. Only do not forget that it is necessary to approach Jesus Christ with the living conscience that you are sinners, that your souls are powerless and dead without Him, and believe wholeheartedly that He is your Creator and Judge, and Only He possesses *the power on earth to forgive sins* (Mark 2:10). Also, do not forget that once you are healed from your spiritual paralysis, it is reckless and dangerous to fall deliberately into a new paralysis. *'See, you have been made well,'* says the Lord. *'Sin no more, lest a worse thing come upon you'* (John 5:14). Amen.

HOMILY 20

On the Second Sunday
of Great Lent

Son, your sins are forgiven you. (Mark 2:5)

Today, beloved children and brethren in Christ, we read the Gospel passage about how our Saviour forgave the sins of the man who was a paralytic in soul and body, who was lowered down by four men from the rooftop of the house where Jesus Christ was preaching and placed before His feet. *'Son, your sins are forgiven you,'* said the Lord to him from the abyss of His mercy. Some of the scribes were also at this house, and they thought within their hearts: why does this man blaspheme so? Who can forgive sins but God alone? How pitiful and thoughtless they were, who despite witnessing the great miracles performed by the Saviour Himself, due to their own pride and malice, did not believe that He is the God-Man and entertained thoughts unworthy of Him. And immediately when Jesus perceived in his spirit that they so reasoned within themselves, He said unto them, *Why do you reason about these things in your hearts? Which is easier to say to the paralytic: 'Your sins are forgiven you,' or to say, 'Arise, and take up your bed, and walk'? But that you may know that the Son of man has power on earth to forgive sins* (he said to the paralytic), *I say to you, Arise, and take up your bed, and go to your house. Immediately he arose, took up the bed, and went out in the presence of them all, so that all were amazed and glorified God, saying, 'We never saw anything like this!'* (Mark 2:1–12). These words conclude today's Gospel reading.

The Holy Church, opportunely and so as to greatly edify, appointed that this Gospel be read on the second Sunday of Great Lent, after a great many of us have already had the opportunity to listen after confession to the same, sweetest voice of the Lord in our souls: *Son, your sins are forgiven you*, for it is the Lord Himself who stands here invisibly during confession, and after forgiving those who are infirm, absolves the sins of those sinners who sincerely repent and confess their sins before the priest. Here I would like to call your attention, brothers and sisters, to the great and solemn mercy of God toward us, repentant sinners, and to the stony insensibility many sinners have toward this wonderful divine mercy shown to them, sinners, of whom I am first, who even after confession and the communion of the Body and Blood of Christ continue to commit the same, and sometimes even worse, sins.

God's immense mercy toward repentant sinners is great and incomprehensible. For us to see more clearly just how immense this mercy is, let us consider, what is sin? Sin is a revolt, a rebellion of the creature against the Creator, disobedience to the Creator, treason against Him, usurping the divine dignity for oneself, or self-adoration: *you will be like god* (Gen 3:5), whispered the snake in the ears of Eve, as today it whispers to the sinner. Sin is a perversion of one's nature, voluntary madness, abominable foolishness, a voluntary turning away from good to evil, from truth to falsehood, from simplicity to malice, from light to darkness, from strength to infirmity, from freedom to captivity, from peace to confusion, from life to death; sin is a disgusting filth, an illusion abominable to God, a poison that corrupts the soul. Sin begot all of the disasters in the world and all diseases, such as the one that afflicted the paralytic mentioned today; it begot all famines, all lethal or epidemic diseases, wars, fires, earthquakes, and all death, both temporary and eternal. Sin turned the highest of the angels into the devil, Lucifer into Satan, as well as all of the spirits who revolted against God, who were once angels of indescribable light and beauty, and became the darkest and most repulsive demons. Sin produced and produces horrible evils, terrible disasters, atrocious upheavals in the world, among mankind; because of sin, all of nature lies in disarray.

It is impossible to describe, impossible to mourn enough, all of the tears of mankind are not enough to grieve for the frightful consequences of sin to the world. If the mercy of the Son of God, through the goodwill of God the Father and the intercession of the Holy Spirit, did not seek out lost sinners, what would have happened to all of us, to all people? It is terrible just to think of it, not to mention to experience even for a minute, for a second, the anguish, the torments that would have befallen outcast sinners: they would have been consumed by the terrible, scorching, unquenchable, eternal flames of hell. But the Son of man, the Son of God, came to recover and *save that which was lost* (Matt 18:11). And so we have been recovered and are being saved: the doors of mercy have been opened to us. Let everyone come with his soul, dejected by sins, to the minister of God; repent sincerely, have heartfelt compunction for your sins, despise them, hate them with all your soul, of which they are worthy, have the firm intention to correct yourself, believe in Christ, the Lamb of God Who takes away the sins of the world, and you will hear the longed-for voice of the Lord: *son, your sins are forgiven you*. And together with the forgiveness of sins you are also delivered from condemnation for them, from the eternal torments prepared for unrepentant sinners, only *go and sin no more*

(John 8:11). Furthermore, if you still sin due to your weakness and evil habits, because *the imagination of man's heart is evil from his youth* (Gen 8:21), and if you once again repent sincerely, then you will once again receive forgiveness, according to the words of the Apostle: *if anyone sins, we have an Advocate with the Father, Jesus Christ the righteous. And He Himself is the propitiation for our sins, and not for ours only but also for the whole world* (1 John 2:1–2). Seventy times seven did the Lord command us to forgive those who fall into sin, for just as He is unmatched, boundless, incomparable, so also is His mercy infinite.

But do we make use of the immense mercy of God with gratitude? Do we correct ourselves? Do we become better day after day, or year after year? Do we strive for perfection, as the Lord commands us: *Therefore you shall be perfect, just as your Father in heaven is perfect* (Matt 5:48). Do we try to see sin in all its hideous nakedness? Do we remove the guise with which it is always trying to cover itself so as not to repel us from it? No, brethren, to our shame we must confess that day in and day out we misuse God's mercy, and after repentance we once again add sin unto sin, *see then that you walk circumspectly* (Eph 5:15); without care we often walk toward sin, and quite often we fall into even greater sins. Where is our reason? Where is our faith? Where is our repentance? It's as if all went away with the dust. Therefore, Satan laughs at us and applauds us. But see, at some point our treachery will come to an end, and we, having tempted God's mercy so many times, will finally experience his terrible judgment. *For it is impossible*, says the holy Apostle Paul, *for those who were once enlightened, and have tasted of the heavenly gift, and have become partakers of the Holy Spirit, and have tasted the good word of God, and the powers of the age to come, if they fall away, to renew them again to repentance; since they crucify again for themselves the Son of God, and put Him to an open shame.... But if it bears thorns and briers, it is rejected and near to being cursed, whose end is to be burned* (Heb 6:4–6, 8).

For if we sin willfully, says the same Apostle, *after we have received the knowledge of the truth, there no longer remains a sacrifice for sins, but a certain fearful expectation of judgment, and fiery indignation which will devour the adversaries. Anyone who has rejected Moses' law dies without mercy on the testimony of two or three witnesses. Of how much worse punishment, do you suppose, will he be thought worthy who has trampled the Son of God underfoot, counted the blood of the covenant by which he was sanctified a common thing, and insulted the Spirit of grace? For we know Him who said, 'Vengeance is mine, I will repay,' says the Lord. And again, 'The Lord will judge His people'* (Heb 10:26–30).

Therefore, my brethren, let us make use of the infinite mercy of God for our salvation, and let us fear to abuse it, so that we will not perish eternally. Amen.

On the Third Sunday of Great Lent

To lighten the ascetic burden of the Fast, the Holy Church established the bringing out of the Life-giving Cross of the Lord in the middle of Lent. He who truly fasts must inevitably endure the tribulations of the flesh, its bitter struggle with the spirit, and, to top it all, the machinations of the devil, acting on our spirit through different thoughts, inspiring great sorrows, especially upon those who are not yet firm, and are imperfect in the Christian life. Therefore, let those who struggle be consoled by the life-giving cross of the Lord, brought out now for veneration and sincere contemplation, and may it lighten their burden. And may none be deprived of its consolation, neither those who do not truly fast, nor those who do not fast at all; let everyone approach it with faith and love, and may they kiss in it the Saviour. Let the divine Sufferer teach everyone from His cross this important duty of the Christian: fasting and the mortification of our sin-loving flesh.

Because the cross itself evokes words of love, let us speak now of the greatness of God's love toward us revealed on the cross, in order to inspire in the cold hearts of Christians' love for God and a life worthy of a Christian.

In fact, what an abyss of love did the Creator reveal on the cross toward His creature, man. The Creator of heaven and earth, of all things visible and invisible; He, Who lit the sky with the sun, the moon, and countless stars; He, Who poured air for the breathing of all that lives, Who poured water on the face of the earth, Who covered all of the earth with vegetation and engenders, raises, and nourishes all living creatures; He, the Only Begotten Son of God, willed to become man for the salvation of men, who had fallen from life to death out of their own volition; He suffered for man the most painful sufferings on the cross, and the most awful death, so that His suffering would be imputed by the just Heavenly Father as the sufferings of all mankind, of all times and places, and so that, in this way, all men devoted to Him with faith and love would be saved from the unimaginable eternal torments in hell, and from a second spiritual death. Man, seeing, with the unclouded eyes of his heart, such great and infinite love of the Omnipotent God for sinful mankind, cannot help but weep, feeling the boundless love of God, and shed tears of love and gratitude, having nothing greater to offer other than his tears for Him Who cherishes our tears of love. However, how do most of us respond to this love God has for us? With insensibility, with a readiness to crucify the Son of God a second time with all possible vices, with an increased servitude to our sinful flesh, so that, most of us, as if oblivious to the sufferings on the cross endured by our Lord Jesus Christ, live neither for heaven nor for our own soul, but live for what is earthly and for the body, and just barely, according to the Church's direction, agree to deprive our flesh of excessive food and drink for a few days.

We try, by all means, to flee from our salvation. The Saviour suffered for us on the cross, but we do not want to know about these sufferings; He commanded that, for our salvation, each of us must take his cross and follow Him toward heavenly glory, and yet we don't want to hear any of it; it was pointed out to us that the mortification of our flesh with its passions and lusts is a remedy for the soul, but we try even harder to satisfy our passions and fulfill our lusts. What then? Such will be our end. And we will be consumed by the eternal fire, and will not receive a single drop of consolation in the fire of Gehenna, because in this life we had all consolations possible, all possible pleasures for our sinful flesh. May God forbid it! Let us rather choose the cross, while the Crucified One still shows us His mercy. Amen.

On the Sunday
of the Veneration of the Cross

Today, beloved brothers and sisters, with God's help I offer you a discussion on the present reading from the Apostle. In it the Apostle Paul speaks about the great High-Priest Who came down from heaven, Jesus, the Son of God, and exhorts us to hold fast to our confession of faith, that is, not to succumb to temptations, sorrows, and persecutions for our faith, because we do not have a High-Priest Who is incapable of suffering together with us in our afflictions; rather we have a High-Priest Who, like us, was tempted in all things, except sin, and as *He Himself has suffered, being tempted, He is able to aid those who are tempted* (Heb 2:18). Next, the Apostle assures us *to come boldly to the throne of grace, that we may obtain mercy and find grace to help in time of need* (Heb 4:16). And what do you do, brothers and sisters, if not precisely this, when you frequently gather together in this temple for communal prayer, or to repent of your sins and commune of the Holy Mysteries, as the Apostle exhorts us in today's reading?

You approach the throne of grace with faith and hope to receive from the Lord mercy, the forgiveness of sins in repentance, and through the communion of the divine Mysteries of the Body and Blood of the Lord, sanctification, fortification for your lives or your future ascetic efforts, and the deification of your souls. Approach, brothers and sisters, approach the throne of grace more and more often, so that you may be granted great and abundant mercy from Him Who sits on the throne, the All-Good and Almighty, the eternal King and High-Priest, our Lord Jesus Christ. But approach God more through earthly priests, men chosen to serve God for you, to bring offerings and sacrifices for sins; resort to their prayerful mediation between you and God and to the sacrifices performed by them, for they bear upon themselves the dignity of the eternal High-Priest Jesus Christ and perform His works for you; oh, but may God permit that they always perform them sincerely, with zeal and reverence, for they do not receive the honor of the priesthood by themselves, but according to a calling from God, as once did the High-Priest Aaron in the Old Testament. Honor them and love them for their dignity, for their most lofty ministry, loftier than all earthly ministries, for their saving and mediating ministry created by God, which brings souls, created according to

His image, to God and to eternal life. God did not make holy angels, bright, menacing, powerful, to be your mediators and performers of the heavenly Mysteries; instead He made people like you, covered, like you, in infirmities and sins, and because of this able to have compassion for your weakness and transgressions, common to all of you.

This is what the Apostle speaks about in today's reading, among other things: *For every high priest taken from among men is appointed for men in things pertaining to God, that he may offer both gifts and sacrifices for sins. He can have compassion on those who are ignorant and going astray, since he himself is also subject to weakness. Because of this he is required as for the people, so also for himself, to offer sacrifices for sins. And no man takes this honor to himself, but he who is called by God, just as Aaron was. So also Christ did not glorify Himself to become High Priest; but it was He who said to Him: 'You are my Son, Today I have begotten You.' As He also says in another place: 'You are a priest forever According to the order of Melchizedek': who, in the days of His flesh, when He had offered up prayers and supplications, with vehement cries and tears to Him who was able to save Him from death, and was heard because of His godly fear, though he was a Son, yet He learned obedience by the things which He suffered. And having been perfected, He became the author of eternal salvation to all who obey Him, called by God as High Priest 'according to the order of Melchizedek'* (Heb 5:1–10).

These are the contents of today's epistle reading, together with their interpretation, teachings, and edifying application for us. In it, I repeat, it is spoken of the only and eternal High Priest, our Lord Jesus Christ, Who before the creation of the world determined to offer Himself on the altar of the cross as a sacrifice of propitiation for the sins of the world, of all people. He offered Himself, according to His Own will, as a sacrifice to God, His Father, for our sins and for propitiation for us, who sin countlessly every day and hour; and we, earthly beings, priests covered in infirmities, bear the dignity of Christ, and through the grace of His Holy Spirit continue to perform His awesome and saving work of reconciliation between God and men; and He Himself, through us, offers in propitiation the awesome and life-giving sacrifice of His Body and Blood on the altar. Always have reverence for this sacrifice and for those who offer it to the Lord; pray also for us, His servants, in your prayers and intercessions; remember His cross, His tomb, His resurrection after three days and His ascension to heaven, and His terrible second coming, and let each and every one take up his cross and follow Him, crucifying his flesh with its passions and lusts. Amen.

HOMILY 23

On the Sunday
of the Veneration of the Cross

Because the cross of the Lord, whose power is often glorified in liturgical prayers and hymns, stands now before our eyes for pious worship and veneration, I would like, beloved, to say a few words about its power, or its miracles. With the intention to speak about this, I, on the one hand, see everywhere its miraculous power, and do not know on what aspect I should tarry longer, which incident to provide as an example of its life-giving power. I see the great veneration that ancient people devoted to the cross; on the other hand, alas, I see very few experiences of its power among our contemporaries. Immediately I see the reason it shows its strength so rarely today, the same reason the Lord performed so few miracles in His homeland, that is, because of ignorance, of lawlessness, of the unchristian way of life of the Christians. Beloved brothers and sisters, the history of the Christian Church provides a great many examples of the life-giving power of the cross, and that is because then people had more faith, there were more true Christians. The life-giving cross is gloriously glorified also in our time, but today we see fewer and fewer examples of its miraculous power, and only among those few people who live with faith.

Christ's holy ascetics were constantly amazed at the life-giving power of the cross of the Lord, which acted in their lives, and in the humility of their hearts, and so that such power would not leave them, frail and sinful, always surrounded by invisible enemies, and often visible ones as well, prayed thus with trembling: "invincible, incomprehensible, divine power of the precious and life-giving cross do not leave us, sinners." With complete faith in its miraculousness, and awed by its power to expel invisible enemies, they invoked the cross with joy in their hearts: "Rejoice, most precious and life-giving cross of the Lord, for Thou drivest away the demons by the power of our Lord Jesus Christ Who was crucified on thee ... and gave us thee, His precious cross, for the driving away of every adversary" ... and without a shadow of a doubt exclaimed to it, as to someone living: "O most precious and life-giving cross of the Lord, help me together with the holy Lady Theotokos, and with all the saints unto the ages."

Our hearts are involuntarily moved when we read with what praise they magnified the life-giving cross.

They called it the power on four ends, all-powerful cross, the glory of the Apostles, the fortitude of the martyrs, the stronghold of reverend men, health of the infirm, the resurrection of the dead, correction of those falling, mortification of the passions, the expulsion of impure thoughts, the foundation of piety, the destruction of demons, the ruin of impure people, the infamy of the enemies on the terrible day of judgment. As alive they called on it: "Oh, cross! Be for me strength, fortitude, and power, a deliverer and the leading soldier against enemies who war against me, a shield and guard, my victory and stronghold, always protecting and preserving me."

They called the image of the cross indescribable by its power, the sanctification of water, purification of the air, sanctification and illumination of every believing Christian, a sign of the courage and the scepter of Christ, which tramples all enemies to the ground. Not knowing how to worthily glorify its power, they exclaimed: "Who can number all of your actions, oh cross, kind to the world, who can number all of your powers and miracles, and all of the dead who have been resurrected by you? You, who have raised up with yourself all of the world, that is, the chosen Christians, raise us up to God."

Do you find the cross of the Lord to be for yourselves, beloved brethren, the same as it was for those holy men?

For the majority of you, I can tell that the answer is no. The cross does not perform miracles in your life. Why? Because of your lack of faith. The cross is in itself always miraculous and life-giving. For Christians who are true to the cross by their faith and piety, so is the cross true to them, as the most faithful and constant friend. Oh! Who will give me divine zeal and the power of words to arouse in the Christians of our time a living faith and the reverence due to it and to the One crucified on it? I know that many are inattentive to the cross and to the sign of the cross. Sometimes this carelessness and lack of respect for the cross reach such a point that they do not receive in their houses those servants of Christ who bear the cross and who come in its name. Others do not want to sign their sinful bodies with the sign of the cross as they should, or they refuse to receive a priestly blessing; sometimes they do receive a blessing inadvertently, but sometimes—oh horror!—from false and damned shame. Are you ashamed of the cross, beloved, which is our praise and our glory? I warn you beforehand: *of him the Son of Man also will be ashamed when He comes in the glory of His Father with the holy angels* (Mark 8:38).

Beloved! Let us always honor the cross of the Lord with faith and love, and it will be our friend, our Saviour, not according to its own power, but because of the power of the Crucified One. Amen.

On the Friday of the Week
of the Veneration of the Cross

*But God forbid that I should boast except in the cross of our
Lord Jesus Christ.* (Gal 6:14)

Last time we heard, beloved, with what praise the
holy men of God spoke regarding the cross. Now,
together with them and the Apostle, I, a great sinner,
would like to glory in the power of the life-giving cross,
for is it possible for a priest, who performs all of the services and mysteries through the power, and with the participation of the cross, to not have experienced in himself
its saving power? *For it* [the cross] *is the power of God to
salvation for everyone who believes* (Rom 1:16). And I would
be very ungrateful to my Saviour and Lord if I remained
silent before those gathered here in church about the
wonderful power of His cross, which has so often displayed, and continues to display, its power on me: *It is
noble to keep hidden the secret of a king, but glorious to*

137

unveil the works of God (Tob 12:7). In fact, by whose power am I, a weak and great sinner, preserved and able to see? By the power of the cross. Who protects me from the enemies visible and invisible that war against me? The cross. Who is my helper in the fight against the passions? *From my youth do many passions war against me* (Matins Antiphon of the 4th tone). The cross of the Lord. The cross protects me from enemies. The beloved Christian who wishes to live piously in Jesus Christ is always persecuted, if not openly, then inwardly, and often both.

But it would be strange to listen from the lips of the priest, and for the priest himself to say, that he does not want to live piously; because the priest must try more than anyone else to live piously. Thus, *all who desire to live godly in Christ Jesus*, according to the words of Scripture, *will suffer persecution* (2 Tim 3:12). I am not talking about exterior enemies. They are easier to conquer precisely because they are visible; when they persecute you, simply remember with faith what Christ suffered for our sake, and then it will be easy to endure their persecution. It is not possible to suffer from the enemies within, the demons, in silence: *For we do not wrestle against flesh and blood, but against principalities, against powers, against the rulers of the darkness of this age, against spiritual hosts of wickedness in the heavenly places* (Eph 6:12); their persecution is always extremely evil, precise, poisonous, and deadly. Moreover, it takes place within, in the heart of man. What can the Christian do? How can he expel the invisible enemies that occupy his very heart? No material weapon is able to expel them from the heart. Moreover, the torments they cause are extremely painful to the soul, a fire, mercilessly devouring his insides. With what means can he expel them and instantly destroy the torments caused by them? With the cross of the Lord, or by making the sign of the life-giving cross over one's chest or body with a living faith in the One crucified on it. As soon as you raise your hand, suddenly the interior torments disappear, and the demons flee. And then one involuntarily exclaims with joy: *rejoice, most-precious and life-giving cross of the Lord, for thou drivest away the demons by the power of our Lord Jesus Christ Who was crucified on thee* (Prayer to the Holy and Precious Cross).

And many times have I, lowly and sinful, expelled from myself the invisible enemies this way. If any passion attaches itself to my heart, and I immediately turn my gaze to Christ and with a living faith I make the sign of the cross over myself, the passion immediately disappears, and the internal fire, the inseparable companion of every passion, also disappears. However, sometimes, alas, the passions captivate me for some time, and only the internal torments I suffer from them force me to sincerely turn to Christ and to His life-giving cross. Therefore, beloved, the cross is my victory over the invisible enemies. Where I cannot penetrate so as to expel them, there penetrates my Christ in the form of His cross and wins the victory I desired. The Lord is wonderful within me, wonderful His life-giving cross! *My strength is made perfect in weakness* (2 Cor 12:9). The invisible enemies, invisibly and mercilessly piercing my soul with their flaming arrows, killing my soul with sorrows and captivity, flee from the name of Jesus Christ and the sign of the cross, terrifying for them; it scorches them as they scorched me, and the Lord returns them what they had caused me. Suddenly lightness fills my soul and it becomes clear, as if after threatening and gloomy clouds.

Let us, beloved brothers and sisters, make the sign of the cross over ourselves, and it will always be our shield and protector. Amen.

On the Sunday
of the Veneration of the Cross

We venerate Thy cross, O Master, and we worship Thy holy resurrection. (Troparion to the Holy Cross)

What does the Holy Church have in mind when it brings out the life-giving cross of the Lord from the altar and offers it to the faithful for veneration? The idea that its true children, who are journeying through the arena of the fast and struggling against their passionate flesh and the devil, who especially during the time of the fast kindles the flames of his arrows in their flesh, may look upon the cross and vividly imagine the suffering of our Lord Jesus Christ, Who for our salvation underwent this suffering in His most-pure flesh, and so that thus they may strengthen themselves in the struggle against their own flesh, with its passions and lusts, and so that they may not regret crucifying it in its passions and courageously take up arms against the enemy, who attacks us with his manifold temptations. It is as if the Lord is telling us from the cross: "Look at what I have suffered for you, what I endured for the sake of your salvation in my immaculate flesh, untouched by any sin; do you refuse to crucify in your own flesh your various passions and lusts? Will you not bear the bitterness of the fast? Will you not tolerate the temporary deprivation of pleasures in order to tame the flesh that, the more you give pleasure to and satisfy, the more possessed it becomes? Will you not bear the fiery arrows of the enemy, when I myself allowed him to pierce My divine flesh with all sorts of arrows?" It is with this thought in mind that the cross is brought out for the veneration of the faithful. Therefore, do not be discouraged from the fast and from the struggle against the passions and the devil, but fight bravely, calling on the help of Him who suffered for us and who through the cross was victorious over our enemies, and be victorious yourselves. Amen.

On the Sunday
of the Veneration of the Cross

Whoever desires to come after Me, let him deny himself, and take up his cross, and follow Me. (Mark 8:34)

The present Sunday of Great Lent is called the week of the veneration of the cross because on this Sunday we venerate the cross and the passion of the Lord of glory, crucified for our sake, and also because on this day the Church has appointed the Gospel reading regarding how each person must bear his own cross, or suffering and sorrows, which in this world are inseparable from the way of following Christ. *Whoever desires to come after Me*, said the Lord to the people and to His disciples, *let him deny himself, and take up his cross, and follow Me. For whoever desires to save his life will lose it, but whoever loses his life*, that is, mortifies all his passions and lusts, *for My sake and the gospel's will save it. For what will it profit a man if he gains the whole world, and loses his own soul?*

Or what will a man give in exchange for his soul? For who-ever is ashamed of Me and My words in this adulterous and sinful generation, of him the Son of Man also will be ashamed when He comes in the glory of His Father with the holy angels (Mark 8:34–38). The Lord Jesus Christ com-mands us to deny ourselves completely, that is, to deny Satan who acts within us, and all his works, and all his service, and all his pride, and to take up our cross, that is, to endure inevitable serious deprivations, infirmities, sufferings, and sorrows, sent to us for our purification, admonition, fortification in the virtues, and to endure the temptations provoked by demons and people. We are extremely attached to our carnal life; we grew accus-tomed to our sins, we have clung to them, and we fear declaring a decisive war against them, breaking all ties with them; we only take half-measures against them, as if protecting ourselves together with them, because it is as if they have become part of our natural traits and therefore we always remain with them. They take root more and more within us, and waging war against them becomes harder and harder; we often lose ourselves to God and become daily the prey and property of the enemy.

The words of the Lord, *whoever desires to save his life will lose it*, are fulfilled in us every day. Every day we sell ourselves to our enemy through all forms of sin living and acting within us; we die spiritually daily, and if only we also rose again every day and returned to life with God through tearful repentance! For *your iniquities have separated you* temporarily *from your God* (Isa 59:2). They can also separate us eternally and forever if we do not turn back and repent wholeheartedly. However, look at the examples of many sinners who became saints: Peter, the publican, Mary of Egypt, Eudoxia, and others. Look at the example of the saints, how they decisively and irrevocably waged war against sin, against the passions, against the devil; how sincerely they loved God and His truth and, renouncing carnal life for the sake of Christ and the Gospel, they saved their souls for all eternity. Why do we not choose to struggle decisively against sin? We love our temporary lives too much, we fear to grieve the flesh, we fear strong temptations, we love the world and its goods too much, forgetting the inevitability of death and the passage to our new life. We count on living long years in constant prosperity; in the pursuit of sensible pleasures we forget the divine nobility of our soul, its predestination for immortality and blessedness. We forget that it is infinitely more precious than the whole world with all of its treasures, which, like a shadow, will pass away. Denouncing such foolish behavior on our part, the Lord says: *For what will it profit a man if he gains the whole world, and loses his own soul? Or what will a man give in exchange for his soul?* (Mark 8:36–37).

There is another reason we do not choose to decisively leave our sinful way of life and remain slaves of the world and its habits, its customs, and all that pertains to this secular, vain life. It is because many of us secretly are ashamed of our faith, are ashamed of confessing the Lord, of living according to His commandments, to His Gospel, to follow Him, so that we will not lose respect and honor in this sinful and adulterous world; and so we allow ourselves to get carried away in the flow of this earthly, sinful, vain, and often most foolish and harmful life. We are aware that we spend our time, which is so precious, recklessly, to our own detriment; we also know what is the highest purpose for man's life on earth, we know about the sacrifice of redemption offered for us on the cross, but the prevalent way of life, our concept of light, our peculiar perverse views on life, on faith, on the Church, do not allow us to withdraw from the crossroads on which we have placed ourselves, and do not allow us to regain consciousness and come to our senses, to think about our fate. We are pitiful slaves of our environment, slaves of the sinful world that lies in evil. However, if you, Christian, wish to follow Christ and to enter into His glory, then you must follow Him without fail, fulfill His commandments, humble yourself, pray, love Him, suffer, and have patience. *By your patience possess your souls* (Luke 21:19).

A terrible retribution awaits unfaithful Christians because they rejected the great care God has shown them and the sacrifice of the Lord Jesus Christ, offered also for them on the cross. They were ashamed of Him, of His Gospel, of living a life according to the Gospel. He will also be ashamed of them when He comes to judge the world in the glory of His Father. He will not recognize them as His own, and will cast them away from His countenance for all eternity. *For whoever is ashamed of Me and My words*, says the Lord, *in this adulterous and sinful generation, of him the Son of Man also will be ashamed when he comes in the glory of His Father with the holy angels* (Mark 8:38). What a terrible fate! Thus, while we still have time, let us renounce the passions, the lusts of the flesh, the lust of the eye, and the pride of life, and let us not fear the cross that leads us to eternal glory, and let us permanently follow Christ wherever He commands us: *and where I am, there My servant will be also* (John 12:26). Amen.

On the Fourth Sunday of Great Lent

Today, beloved brothers and sisters, was read the Gospel passage from the Evangelist Mark on how a father asked Jesus Christ to heal his son, a deaf and dumb child who was possessed, by casting out the evil spirit who was the reason the child was deaf and dumb. *'Deaf and dumb spirit,'* said the Lord to the impure one, *'I command you, come out of him and enter him no more.' Then the spirit cried out, convulsed him greatly, and came out of him. And he became as one dead, so that many said, 'He is dead.' But Jesus took him by the hand and lifted him up, and he arose* (Mark 9:25–27). But see how evil was the spirit who tormented the child. His father told the Lord how *wherever it seizes him, it throws him down; he foams at the mouth, gnashes his teeth, and becomes rigid* (Mark 9:18). This happened also at the time when the father brought his son to the Saviour. And when the Lord asked the father, as if he did not already know, even though, as God, He knows all, *'How long has this been happening to him?'* And he said, *'From childhood. And often he has thrown him both into the fire and into the water to destroy him,'* and he asked the Lord to have compassion on him and his son, and to help them, if He can do anything. Jesus told him: *'If you can believe, all things are possible to him who believes.'* And the unfortunate father of little faith cried out with tears *'Lord, I believe; help my unbelief!'* (Mark 9:21–24).

Do you see what power the Lord attributes to faith and to the one who believes? *All things are possible to him who believes,* He says. The one who believes is able to cast out demons and to heal all kinds of diseases. And how powerless and miserable is the unbeliever! He cannot even control himself, and cannot overcome his own sins, but as a slave he serves them and is tormented by them. And as the unfortunate father initially brought his possessed son to the Apostles and they were not able to expel this demon from him, they asked the Lord in private why they were not able to expel him. The Lord answered them: *This kind can come out by nothing but prayer and fasting* (Mark 9:29). Such is the Lord's praise for prayer and fasting. This is the evangelical basis for fasting. How could those who call themselves followers of the Gospel have expelled fasting from our common life, as if it was unnecessary?! Is it not because in our days passions and iniquity and demonic possessions of all kinds have multiplied, so much so that some Christians have broken their ties with the Church and have renounced prayer and fasting as something superfluous? And they live like dumb beasts, guided solely by their various lusts, while others, due to their malice, foam at the mouth like men truly possessed, intent on committing every evil deed: murder, suicide, arson, placing mines, causing explosions, and so on.

Yes, beloved brothers and sisters, such people have reached such a terrible frenzy precisely because of their unbelief, intemperance, impurity, and from all of the ruinous consequences of this unbelief. The meek faith of the Gospel does not preach murder, regicide, placing mines, and causing explosions; it says: *Let every soul be subject to the governing authorities. For there is no authority except from God, and the authorities that exist are appointed by God*, and it is necessary to be subject unto them *not only because of wrath but also for conscience's sake* (Rom 13:1, 5), and it commands us to pray *for kings and all who are in authority, that we may lead a quiet and peaceable life in all godliness and reverence* (1 Tim 2:2). Lord, illumine the eyes of the hearts, blinded with malice, of these miserable possessed people of our unfortunate times, who rise up against the authority appointed by God, let them know what a terrible abyss they dig under their own selves, and into what a terrible hellish pit they are about to plunge.

In ancient, pre-Christian times, some unfortunate Hebrews revolted against the established authority, against Moses and Aaron, reproaching them for an alleged love of power, only murmuring against them; and what came of it, what was God's punishment? The earth opened up underneath them, and they went down alive into the pit of hell together with their families, while others, not as guilty as those, were consumed by a fire that came from the temple (Num 16:1–35). See what a terrible sin it is to revolt against those in authority! What then awaits our nihilists, what will be the judgment of God? The greater the gifts of God they trample upon, so much more terrible will be God's judgment. For who are our nihilists and terrorists? Baptized people, Christians, committing such acts of violence, such murders and suicides, such satanic villainy! Oh, why were they born? Why did they not perish in their mothers' womb? It would have been better had they never been born. To trample so ungratefully, viciously, madly on God's gifts: on the grace of baptism, of chrismation, of the communion of the Lord's Body and Blood, is something truly terrible! Oh, hapless parents of such children! What shame must they suffer!

Brothers and sisters! Let us hold onto the faith of God's Church wholeheartedly, onto this unique saving ark that saves us from the fiery universal flood that will befall all transgressors in due time. Let us hold onto the holy precepts of the Church, leading us to salvation, let us observe unwaveringly fasting and prayer, and be zealous to serve God. *The devil*, the enemy of our salvation, does not sleep, but *walks about like a roaring lion* around us, *seeking whom he may devour* (1 Pet 5:8), and how many has he already devoured! Fasting and prayer observed with zeal, with humility, with faith and love, are powerful weapons against the devil and against all of the passions that war within us. Amen.

HOMILY 28

On the Fifth Sunday
of Great Lent

Beloved brothers and sisters! I would like to tell you now and somewhat expound on today's readings from the Epistle and the Gospel. Today we listened to a passage from the Apostle Paul's epistle to the Hebrews regarding the cleansing power of the blood of Christ our Saviour, Who offered Himself as a sacrifice to God the Father for the sins of all (Heb 9:11–14); and we listened to the passage from the Gospel of the Evangelist Mark regarding how our Lord Jesus Christ foretold in advance to His twelve Apostles, including Judas the traitor, how He, our Lord, *will be betrayed to the chief priests and to the scribes; and they will condemn Him to death and deliver Him to the Gentiles; and they will mock Him, and scourge Him, and spit on Him, and kill Him. And the third day He will rise again* (Mark 10:33–34). Later in the Gospel we listened to the inappropriate request of two of the disciples, the brothers John and James, to sit in the

153

first places when Jesus Christ is glorified, and how the Lord gently rebuked them, saying that the way to His glory is the way of the cross, of suffering, and death; the indignation of the other disciples with John and James's pretension, and the commandment the Lord gave to all regarding this matter: *whoever desires to become great among you shall be your servant. And whoever of you desires to be first shall be slave of all. For even the Son of Man did not come to be served, but to serve, and to give His life a ransom for many* (Mark 10:32–45).

Let us now return to the Epistle reading. In his epistle to the Hebrews, the Apostle Paul speaks of how *Christ came as High Priest of the good things to come, with the greater and more perfect tabernacle not made with hands, that is, not of this creation. Not with the blood of goats and calves, but with His own blood He entered the Most Holy Place once for all, having obtained eternal redemption. For if the blood of bulls and goats and the ashes of a heifer, sprinkling the unclean, sanctifies for the purifying of the flesh, how much more shall the blood of Christ, who through the eternal Spirit offered Himself without a spot to God, cleanse your conscience from dead works to serve the living God* (Heb 9:11–14). Therefore, the meaning of the apostolic reading is that if the prefigurative blood of the old covenant, the blood of sacrificed animals, sanctified those who were unclean, so that their bodies would be cleansed, then how much more will the blood of Christ cleanse our conscience, soul and body, from all sin. And the Apostle John the Theologian says that *the blood of Jesus Christ His Son cleanses us from all sin* (1 John 1:7). So, let no one among the sinners despair, no matter how sinful he may be, but let him hope to receive the forgiveness and purification of all his sins, for we have the Saviour, Who according to His grace is always present with us in His Church, especially in the Holy Mysteries, Who comes down to cleanse from all sin if we but believe in Him, and sincerely and firmly repent and commune with faith and love of His Most-Pure Body and Blood.

Let us now remember St Mary of Egypt, who initially was sunk in the abyss of evil, in the depths of depravity; but repentance, faith, and love, the ascetical struggles of fasting and prayer, and the communion of Christ's Holy Mysteries purified her, made her holy and equal to the angels. Let us imitate her faith, her diligence in repentance and prayer and love of God, her thirst for the communion of Christ's Body and Blood, and the Lord will cleanse us of all sin, *for with the Lord there is mercy. And with Him is abundant redemption. And He shall redeem* us *from all* our *iniquities* (Ps 130: 7–8). In today's Gospel, our Lord Jesus Christ teaches us that we should not covet primacy and superiority over others out of ambition and vanity, but that we should strive for the only honor that is pleasing to God, that is, of serving others for salvation, as Christ God Himself *did not come to be served, but to serve, and to give His life a ransom for many. And whoever of you desires to be first shall be slave of all* (Mark 10:45, 44). *Bear one another's burdens, and so fulfill the law of Christ* (Gal 6:2). Amen.

HOMILY 29

On the Fifth Sunday of Great Lent

The Son of man did not come to be served, but to serve, and to give His life a ransom for many. (Mark 10:45)

Soon the memorable days of the salvific suffering of our Lord Jesus Christ will be upon us, and on the present Sunday the Church has appointed the reading of the Gospel passage on which the Lord foretells His coming suffering as real and present. Namely, He said: *Behold, we are going up to Jerusalem, and the Son of Man will be betrayed to the chief priests and to the scribes; and they will condemn Him to death and deliver Him to the Gentiles; and they will mock Him, and scourge Him, and spit on Him, and kill Him. And the third day He will rise again* (Mark 10:33–34). The Lord knew beforehand everything that would happen to Him in Jerusalem, all the details of His humiliation, His suffering and death, and He did not shy away from them, but went readily and willingly to drink the bitter cup of suffering for the whole world, and for the most ungrateful Jews themselves who crucified Him, in order to obtain our common salvation. What boundless love! What immense condescension! What wonderful longsuffering!

All of Jesus Christ's life, from His childhood to the death on the cross and the resurrection, constitute His wonderful, loving ministry for the salvation of the human race. And since His ascension to heaven, when He sat at the right hand of the Father, until today, the Lord reigns over all nations, ministering to the salvation of the human race, especially of Christians, as He Himself said: *Lo, I am with you always, even to the end of the age* (Matt 28:20), or as we read in today's Gospel: *The Son of man did not come to be served, but to serve, and to give His life a ransom for many.* To this day He purifies, revives, and renews us through holy baptism; He sanctifies and confirms us through the grace of the Holy Spirit in chrismation; He celebrates the liturgy as eternal High Priest according to the order of Melchizedek, and grants His Most-Pure Body and Blood in the form of bread and wine. During confession, He Himself receives our repentance and absolves the sins of those who sincerely repent. Through the priesthood, the hierarchy of pastors, He Himself spiritually illumines, shepherds, guides, judges, and punishes His rational sheep. In matrimony, He blesses the conjugal union of husband

and wife for the blessed birth and upbringing of children. During holy unction, as Healer of body and soul, He heals our spiritual and physical infirmities.

In each service He is invisibly present with us, according to His own promise: *where two or three are gathered together in My name, I am there in the midst of them* (Matt 18:20), and He receives our ministry. He Himself wonderfully, effectively, palpably ministers for our salvation, producing in us a remarkable, divine strength that destroys the iron chains and shackles of sin and spiritual death, healing our infirmities, redeeming us of our countless transgressions every day for our repentance and faith, delightfully renewing our souls, worn out from the bitterness of sin.

Right now we are journeying through Great Lent, which lasts for forty days. What is this Great Lent? It is a precious gift from our Saviour, Who Himself fasted for forty days and nights, neither eating nor drinking; it is truly a precious gift for all who desire salvation, as a way to mortify the passions of our soul. Through His words and His example the Lord established it for His followers. And with what love, what divine, grace-filled power the Lord ministers to those who fast truly! He illumines them, purifies them, renews them, strengthens them in the struggle against the passions and invisible enemies, *against principalities, against powers, against the rulers of the darkness of this age* (Eph 6:12). He instructs us in every virtue and raises us to perfection, to incorruption and heavenly bliss. All those who truly fast have felt this, and continue to feel it, within themselves. Fasting united to prayer is a faithful weapon against the devil and our passion-filled flesh. Let no one think that the fast is unnecessary. But behold, the days of suffering of our Sweetest Lord are at hand.

What is the suffering, the passion of the Lord? It is the last, fulfilling sacrifice of our Saviour for the sins of the world, ending with His death on the cross, before which He cried: *It is finished!* (John 19:30). It is His final, definitive ministry on earth for our salvation, so that through His suffering and death we would be delivered from the just and eternal torments for our sins, so that He could give us as food and drink His Most-Pure, Much-Suffering Flesh, and His Most-Pure Blood, shed for us, for our purification, sanctification, vivification, and renewal in order to clothe us in His righteousness, through His own merits, so that we would be deified and enjoy eternal bliss. Ah, if only this were so! If only we always looked upon His sufferings and assimilated them with faith and love! If only we also crucified ourselves together with Him, crucifying the world and its passions!

The liturgy is celebrated almost year round. What is the liturgy? It is the daily ministry of the Lord for our salvation and the salvation of the world—for each and every one. He Himself ministers for us and is with us in the liturgy, performing the Mystery of His Body and Blood. To this day He is pierced for us, Himself remaining whole and incorrupt in His deified flesh. He sheds His Blood and breaks His Body and gives them to us for the remission of sins, for sanctification and eternal life. To this day the warmth of His living and life-giving Blood is felt upon the altars of Orthodox Christian churches! What a wonderful, divine gift of love! What bliss for all true Christians! Thus the Lord to this day ministers diversely and vividly unto our salvation.

But He also left us an image, an example, of how we also should serve one another with love. He said: *but whoever desires to become great among you shall be your servant. And whoever desires to be first shall be slave of all* (Mark 10:43–44). Thus each one of us, my brethren, must serve one another with his talents, his abilities, his strengths, his profession, his patrimony, his education, and not only please himself. Therefore, the tsar and the government serve the people, caring for its education, the direction of their moral and physical strengths, the country's agricultural and economic well-being. Priests must serve their flock, or should serve as good examples of the Christian virtues by word, instructions, and exhortations; by performing the mysteries with reverence; and by guiding their flock toward a virtuous life and salvation in God. Educated people, those in authority, teachers, authors, writers, and printing in general must serve for the glory of God and the benefit of the people, and the leadership entrusted to them must use its educational influence on the basis of the teachings of the Orthodox Church.

People who are rich must serve those who are poor; not parasites, of course, who do not want to work and want to eat their bread for free; for, *if anyone will not work, neither shall he eat* (2 Thess 3:10), says the Apostle, but those poor people who would have wanted to work, but can't, or those whose work is not going well, or who perform exhausting, ungrateful labor, or those who simply cannot find work anywhere. We are all members of one another in Christ and according to our faith, and it is our duty and conviction of heart and mind that we must serve one another, each person however he can. Yes, brethren, to serve our neighbor, and not just live for ourselves, not just live to satisfy our own desires, not gather only for ourselves, not waste our time in idleness and laziness, not think that our life is a game, or that it is just a chain of games and pleasures. That would not be Christianity, but paganism. *We then who are strong ought to bear with the scruples of the weak, and not to please ourselves. Let each of us please his neighbor for his good, leading to edification* (Rom 15:1–2).

Serving one's neighbor, of course, cannot happen without denying oneself and taking up one's cross, and sometimes the more good we do to our neighbor, all the more difficult our cross becomes to bear, for example, the cross of ingratitude and malice from those to whom we do much good. Such is the cross of our good and beloved Sovereign. But one should not despair, or be distressed beyond measure because of this, and give up on serving others. For what cross was more difficult than the cross Christ bore for us? May the example of our Lord Jesus Christ, who exhausted Himself terribly for us, serve as a strong motivation for us to neither fear nor avoid self-denial for the common good. And self-denial and the common good are so necessary, especially now, in light of the great hardship and misery facing our people, who though they are good and believing, they are also uneducated and at time superstitious, dissolute, careless, often short-sighted. Free, and yet they still have not learned to understand and appreciate the gift of true freedom. To sincerely serve our neighbor, it is necessary, without fail, to stop serving our own passions, it is necessary to have self-denial. The passions do not allow us to serve our neighbor sincerely and with zeal, but teach us to please only ourselves. Amen.

On the Hymn "Behold, the Bridegroom Comes at Midnight"

Y ou have now heard, beloved, the moving hymn "Behold, the Bridegroom Comes at Midnight," which is sung at matins during the first three days of Passion Week. So that the hymn will be understood by all, and will bring to all the desired benefit, please allow me to offer your charity an explanation for it. The hymn "Behold, the Bridegroom Comes at Midnight" reminds us of the Saviour's parable in which He compares the kingdom of heaven with ten virgins who, according to an ancient custom, took their lamps and went out to meet the bridegroom. The composer of the hymn had precisely this parable in mind. We present it here and shall explain it briefly. *Then the kingdom of heaven shall be likened to ten virgins,* says the Saviour, *who took their lamps and went out to meet the bridegroom. Now five of them were wise, and five were foolish. Those who were foolish took their lamps and took no oil with them,*

*but the wise took oil in their vessels with their lamps. But
while the bridegroom was delayed, they all slumbered and
slept. And at midnight a cry was heard: 'Behold, the bridegroom is coming; go out to meet him!' Then all those virgins
arose and trimmed their lamps. And the foolish said to the
wise, 'Give us some of your oil, for our lamps are going out.'
But the wise answered, saying, 'No, lest there should not be
enough for us and you; but go rather to those who sell, and
buy for yourselves.' And while they went to buy, the bridegroom came, and those who were ready went in with him
to the wedding; and the door was shut. Afterward the other
virgins came also, saying, 'Lord, Lord, open to us!' But he
answered and said, "Assuredly, I say to you, I do not know
you.' Watch therefore, for you know neither the day nor the
hour in which the Son of Man is coming* (Matt 25:1–13).

The explanation of the parable is as follows: the ten
virgins, of which five were wise and five foolish, sym-
bolize us Christians. Some of us are wise because of our
faith, our virtuous life, and because we are prepared for
our death; others are foolish due to their unbelief or cold
indifference to the faith, their impure carnal life, and
their being unprepared for their death and the judgment that will immediately follow it, for *it is appointed
for men to die once, but after this the judgment* (Heb 9:27).
The foolish ones, it is said, took their lamps but did not
take oil with them. What do the lamps and the oil for
the lamps mean? The lamps are our souls, according

to the Saviour's words: *the lamp of the body is the eye* (Matt 6:22), by "eye" He means the heart of man, or soul. The oil symbolizes alms, according to St John Chrysostom's interpretation, or good deeds in general. Therefore, the foolish Christians, going out to meet the bridegroom, did not prepare for their souls good deeds, which could have supported their spiritual life. The wise ones, it is said, took oil in their vessels with their lamps, meaning that they stocked up on good deeds in order to worthily meet the bridegroom. Who is the bridegroom? Jesus Christ. When and how do we go out to meet Him? Our entire lives must be since their beginning a preparation for our personal meeting with Him, because every soul after its death must appear and answer before Him, as to the Author of our life. Throughout our lives we must take care to acquire and preserve in our hearts a living faith and an ardent love for God, so that after our deaths standing before the terrible throne of the Lord of glory will neither be shameful nor to our condemnation. We will go out for the general meeting with Him during our resurrection from the dead, when *all who are in the graves will hear His voice and come forth—those who have done good, to the resurrection of life, and those who have done evil, to the resurrection of condemnation* (John 5:28–29).

The bridegroom, that is, Jesus Christ, is in no hurry to cut our lives short with death, *not willing that any should perish but that all should come to repentance* (2 Pet 3:9), and is

equally delaying His glorious, and dreadful, second coming so that the sons of the kingdom may multiply more
and more. Meanwhile, people, temporarily seduced by
the sweetness of sin, by its impunity, and seeing that the
world remains stable, think it will remain as such forever, and they themselves, enjoying robust health and
other material goods, immerse themselves in spiritual
slumber, not caring for their correction, and thus sleep
the sleep of sin. However, precisely at the midnight of
their sinful sleep, when none among the sinners thinks
about the grave dangers in which they find themselves,
a loud voice is heard: behold, the bridegroom comes, go
out to meet Him. Then all will tremble and light their
lamps, that is, will exert spiritual attention. At that time
it will be good for the wise Christians: their souls will
ignite with the sweetest love for God; but for the foolish,
it will be bad. Their souls, like lamps without oil, will die
out, that is, they will grow dark and cold from the lack
of love for God, the source of love, and will start to taste
the torments of hell. They will ask the wise Christians
for oil, that is, for good deeds, but those will not give it
to them, so that they also may not be lacking. They will
go and buy oil from those that sell it, that is, they will
suddenly remember to do good deeds, and will look for
opportunities to do them, however, precisely at this time
when they wish to do good deeds, the bridegroom will
come, death will catch them by surprise, and will place

them before the heavenly Judge without any virtues whatsoever, reeking of the filth of their own lawlessness. They will desire to go inside the bridal chamber of the heavenly kingdom, which all of us from birth are destined to enter, the reason for which we live. Their Lord will not allow them to enter, and will say to them: I do not know you. *Watch therefore*, the Lord concludes the parable, *for you know neither the day nor the hour in which the Son of Man is coming*.

Now all of us understand the church hymn: "Behold, the Bridegroom comes at midnight, and blessed is that servant," that is, every Christian, "whom He shall find watching, and again, unworthy is the servant whom He shall find heedless (sleeping the sleep of sin). Beware, therefore, O my soul, do not be weighed down with sleep (that is, do not be weighed down with the sleep of sin), lest you be given up to (eternal) death, and lest you be shut out of the Kingdom. But rouse yourself crying: Holy, holy, holy, art Thou, O our God, through the Theotokos have mercy on us." Amen.

HOMILY 31

On Great Monday

Today, beloved brethren, at matins three parables were read. The first one was about the barren fig tree. The second one was about a father who had two sons and asked each of them to go work in his vineyard: one of them answered that he did not want to do it, but later changed his mind and went; the other answered the same question saying that he would go to work, but did not go. Finally, the third parable: *There was a certain landowner who planted a vineyard and set a hedge around it, dug a winepress in it and built a tower. And he leased it to vinedressers and went into a far country. Now when vintage-time drew near, he sent his servants to the vinedressers that they might receive its fruit. And the vinedressers took his servants, beat one, killed one, and stoned another.... Then last of all he sent his son to them, ... and they cast him out of the vineyard and killed him* (Matt 21:33–39).

Let us discuss now the first parable. Having spent the night in the village of Bethany, in the morning the

Lord, says the Evangelist Matthew, *as He returned to the city, He was hungry. And seeing a fig tree by the road, He came to it and found nothing on it but leaves, and said to it, 'Let no fruit grow on you ever again.' Immediately the fig tree withered away. And when the disciples saw it, they marveled, saying, 'How did the fig tree wither away so soon?' So Jesus answered and said to them, 'Assuredly, I say to you, if you have faith and do not doubt, you will not only do what was done to the fig tree, but also if you say to this mountain, "Be removed and be cast into the sea," it will be done. And whatever things you ask in prayer, believing, you will receive'* (Matt 21:17–22).

The barren fig tree, which had leaves only, is me and you, beloved brothers and sisters. The Planter of our life, our Lord Jesus Christ, often comes to us thirsting for our salvation; early and late He comes to satisfy the hunger of our souls, to become the bread of life for it. And, alas, almost always He finds in us only the cares of this life, only leaves. The fruits of faith, of invincible care for the salvation of our souls, are simply not there. Meanwhile, each of us was planted on this earth with the same goal, to bring forth spiritual fruits. What are the particular fruits each person must bring forth, especially Christians? The Apostle Paul provides the following answer to this: *the fruit of the Spirit is love, joy, peace, longsuffering, kindness, goodness, faithfulness* (Gal 5:22). See, brother and sister, which fruits we must bring daily, without fail, to the Planter of our life, our Lord Jesus Christ? Now let each person consider: are you a fruitful, or barren, fig tree? If you are a fruitful one, good, carry on, bring forth more and more fruits to the Lord so that He may nourish you Himself with them in eternity. If, however, you are a barren fig tree, then tremble; the curse of the Master of your life threatens you and, perhaps very soon, He will tell you: *Let no fruit grow on you ever again.* And you will immediately wither away, all of your spiritual strength will die out, and your faith, hope, and love will dry out completely, and *every tree which does not bear good fruit is cut down and thrown into the* eternal *fire* (Matt 3:10).

These words are true, and clear as the day. They are fulfilled indisputably: *heaven and earth will pass away*, as the days, months, and years pass, *but My words will by no means pass away* (Mark 13:31). Therefore, brother and sister, ask yourself: do you bring forth daily to the Master of your life fruits of good deeds, and more important, do you possess the queen of all virtues, love, ardent love toward your Creator and love for your neighbor as yourself? Do you wish to know by which works love reveals itself? The Apostle Paul will answer you in my stead: *Love suffers long and is kind; love does not envy; love does not parade itself, is not puffed up, does not behave rudely, does not seek its own, is not provoked, thinks no evil; does not rejoice in iniquity, but rejoices in the truth; bears all things, believes all things, hopes all things, endures all things. Love never fails* (1 Cor 13:4–8).

Love is so necessary for the Christian that, even if he speaks in all of the tongues of men and of the angels and does not have love, then he is as a sounding brass despite all of his eloquence and verbosity, or like a tinkling cymbal. If he possesses the gift of prophecy, and understands all mysteries and all knowledge, and even, which is most astonishing of all, if he possesses all faith, so that by his words he can move mountains, and yet does not possess love, then he is nothing; vain is all his repentance, empty works without love (1 Cor 13:1–8). Why is love so necessary to us? Because *God* Himself *is love* (1 John 4:8), and we were made according to His image, and God lives within the Christian. *Do you not know yourselves, that Jesus Christ is in you?—unless indeed you are disqualified* (2 Cor 13:5). *Do you not know that you are the temple of God and that the Spirit of God dwells in you?* (1 Cor 3:16). He who possesses an ardent love for God and neighbor has also within his soul the remaining fruits mentioned by the Apostle, joy in the Holy Spirit, peace, longsuffering, gentleness, mercy, faith. Within love, as within a seed, are contained all the virtues; for where love is, there is God, all-perfect perfection, the source of goodness, infinite blessing, infinite omnipotence. He who possesses ardent love for God possesses also such faith that can move mountains, as the

Lord said: *and whatever things you ask in prayer, believing, you will receive* (Matt 21:22). Therefore, if we do not wish to dry out like the fig tree cursed by the Lord, or like the grass that will be cast into the eternal flame, let us, brothers and sisters, try to bring forth fruits of good deeds to the Planter of our life while we still have time, strength, means, and opportunities. It may be that the time will come when we would have liked to do good, but it will be impossible. *Therefore, as we have opportunity, let us do good to all, especially to those who are of the household of faith* (Gal 6:10). Amen.

On Great Wednesday

Brethren! Today is the day on which our Lord Jesus Christ was betrayed in order to suffer and die for us.

O, faithful souls who are able to appreciate and feel the enormous self-sacrifice for our salvation of our common Lord and friend! From this day on, keep mainly your hearts in the most careful way for Him alone, and do not allow yourselves to be possessed by any worldly, corruptible passion. Prove that you are also able to answer love with love, that you are true Christians, and that out of love for Christ you can keep vigil with Him, that is, you can keep watch over your hearts, even if but for the few hours in which He drank the cup of heavenly wrath prepared for us. Enter within your hearts with faith in the Lord Jesus Christ, who suffered for us, and suffer there, within your hearts, together with Him; remember your sins, repent, and if you can, weep for them. *Weep for yourselves* (Luke 23:28), says the Lord. Send your sighs and tears to Christ, and this will be the most pleasing sacrifice to the Lord Who suffered for us; soon you will feel in your hearts His favor towards you for your heartfelt gift; *peace* in your souls, *which surpasses all understanding* (Phil 4:7). A heavenly, tranquil joy will let you know that your sacrifice of a humbled and contrite heart was not despised, but was accepted by the Lord in His heavenly and noetic altar. Having cleansed yourselves from your sins this evening through the mystery of repentance, if any of you has not yet done so before, you will be worthy to commune of His Body and Blood. This supper of love may unite you to Him Who commanded that it be celebrated in His memory, that it may always remind you of His limitless love for us, and that it may give you strength to spend the coming great days in a holy fashion, in the spirit of ardent love for the Lord, Who laid down His life for us. Amen.

On Great and Holy Friday
Before the Holy Shroud

Behold the man! (John 19:5)

Behold how our sinless and Most-Holy Lord Jesus Christ was insulted, wounded, tormented! What need was there for the dispassionate God to suffer so horribly in His flesh at the hands of the people? What need was there for the God-Man Himself to bear such hellish torments on earth? For God, brethren, there was no need to expose Himself to such dishonor, such torments here on earth. His self-sacrifice was completely voluntary, and He could have not become incarnate, be tormented, or die. Only then, all of us, as sinners and enemies of God, would have remained forever prisoners and slaves of the devil, and all would be lost forever; then there would not be these two sides, left and right, it would not have been said that the righteous will go to eternal life, and sinners, to eternal sufferings: there would be a single, terrible fate for everyone, eternal torments. It is terrifying even to think of it! But the Lord, according to His infinite mercy, could not bear to see mankind suffer at the hands of the devil, and came to free us from this captivity and from eternal torments. And in order to free us from slavery to the enemy, to whom we gave, and give ourselves freely, He wished to become for us, according to the flesh, an obedient servant to His Heavenly Father, to Whom we were, and now are, constantly disobedient, and in human flesh and with a human soul, human strength, reinforced by divinity, to defeat the devil-tempter, to whom we so easily surrendered in captivity, and now also surrender through our sins. Furthermore, He, the pre-eternal God, wished to bear on His Own human essence, to bear Himself the eternal torments due to us, to free us from the eternal torments of hell, which, in all fairness, our eternal souls should have undergone, being slaves to the devil. And thus, as you can see and hear from the Gospel, He suffered these torments for us. He suffered all of the shame and cruel torments from the people and demons to release us from hell, where we should have suffered eternally, were it not for the Saviour.

However, even though Christ released us from hell, we willingly go there fearlessly, with eyes closed, in order not to see the light, in order not to come back to it. Many of us fearlessly give ourselves over to every form of sin, without a single thought of correcting ourselves, as if

Christ were some servant of sin, who guides everyone, even the unrepentant, even those who refuse to change their sinful hearts and deeds to paradise. An unfathomable hard-heartedness and insensitivity rules over many of us. All of creation trembled before the sufferings and death of our Saviour Jesus Christ. The earth quaked, stones turned over, the dead arose, and yet our souls do not tremble with fear before the death of the God-Man, before the remembrance of eternal and cruel torments, which we should have undergone had our Lord not suffered and died for us. Our heart does not break, does not soften, does not part with its lack of faith, unbelief, with its hard-heartedness, pride, with its malice toward our neighbor, its envy of his prosperity, with condemnation, with gluttony, overeating and drunkenness, stinginess, avarice, with carnal impurity. How many such people stand here today before this holy shroud, who even during this sacred and dreadful time do not stop serving the devil and nourishing anger toward his neighbor, who envy one another, think about money, about theft, about drunkenness, about impurity?

How many are there who only wait for the feast and immediately start to engage in drunkenness, and surrender to debauchery, and violate the temple of their body, which formerly was the temple of the Lord through the communion of the holy Mysteries of Christ's body and blood? But why am I talking about the feast? Do we not see this happening even before the feast, even now, when we remember how Christ suffered for us, do we not see people getting drunk and giving themselves over to dissoluteness? They are a lawless people, who now bless Christ with their lips, and tomorrow, or even today, will blaspheme Him with their deeds. Oh, ungrateful, insensitive, foolish, hard-hearted people, who today act as if you suffer with Christ and are crucified together with Him, but tomorrow, or after, will crucify Him! How much longer will we behave like this, brethren? How much longer will we be hypocrites? How much longer will we serve the devil and senselessly offend the Lord? Brethren, if the stones of our heart, with its manifold malice, its passions, its impurity, will not turn over; if we do not remove from them lack of faith, unbelief, coldness, gluttony and drunkenness, dissoluteness, malice, pride, envy, sloth, idleness, and all other passions, then one day those stones that turned over when Christ died will condemn us. If we do not repent and do not turn to God with all our hearts, then we will go to that hell from which the Son of God came to free us. Truthfully, brethren! *Unless you repent you will all likewise perish* (Luke 13:3). *Of how much worse punishment, do you suppose, will he be thought worthy who has trampled the Son of God underfoot, counted the blood of the covenant by which he was sanctified a common thing, and insulted the Spirit of grace? For we know Him who said, 'Vengeance is Mine, I will repay,' says the Lord. And again, 'The Lord will judge His people.' It is a fearful thing to fall into the hands of the living God* (Heb 10: 29–31). Amen.

HOMILY 34

On Great and Holy Friday Before the Holy Shroud

Behold! The Lamb of God who takes away the sin of the world! (John 1:29)

Behold, my brethren, the Lamb of God, Who took upon Himself our sins, my sins, the sins of each one of us. Behold the only-begotten, incarnate Son of God, tortured by men's hatred and evil! What humanity! Oh, what a grim, abominable picture of human malice! Let us fall before Him in confession, and grieve before the Lord Who made us, and Who at the end of the ages suffered and died for us. With fear and love let us fall down, with our hearts and lips, before these wounds. With fear, because to this moment our sins reek and cry out for our punishment; with love, for these wounds and the death were suffered by Him due to His ineffable love for us, and naturally they call upon us to love! *Behold! The Lamb of God who takes away the sin of the world!* How pleasant

these words are to the souls of the faithful! They contain
our strong hope for the infinite mercy of the Heavenly
Father, Who reconciled Himself to us sinners through
the sacrifice of justice, offered on the cross for our sins,
that is, the eternal sacrifice of His Son. How many times
have we sinned in a single day and hour, not to mention
the sins of our entire wretched lives? How much did our
sins torment us? But we repented with faith and sincere
hope, and looked to the Saviour, sighed and grieved for
our sins; and behold, they are cleansed, purified, forgiven.
We have found rest, freedom, joy. What does this mean?
It means that the Lamb of God on each day, at every hour,
throughout all the days of our lives takes away our sins,
removes them, purifies them, forgets them, freeing us
from the eternal condemnation due to them.

Who among us did not experience this within himself? That is why before this bloody, stunning sight we
stand with hope, and though we sorrow, it is a sorrow
filled with compunction, with joy, and some solemnity,
for we are certain that within this Dead Man lies the life
of all the living, reconciliation with God, forgiveness of
sins and hope of life eternal. Today Christians throughout the world worship the wounds of the Saviour with
pious affection, and movingly kiss them, and everywhere all the hearts of the faithful feel the life-giving
power of the salvific sufferings and death of the Lord, for
He continuously and everywhere takes away the sins of

all repentant sinners, has mercy on them, purifies them, renews them, saves them. Oh, our Saviour! From how many spiritual deaths have You saved me and each of us? Oh, my Saviour, today, at this hour, before this pious gathering, I confess Your mercies revealed to me, the worst sinner among men, how You saved me from innumerable spiritual deaths, how You saved and continue to save me from every affliction, from every fall into sin. And it is only through Your mercy that to this day I have not fallen into the pit of destruction, therefore I proclaim, together with the Prophet David: *The sorrows of Sheol surrounded me; The snares of death confronted me. In my distress I called upon the Lord, And cried out to my God* (Ps 18:5–7); and He has always answered with mercy to the sighs of my heart, and has revealed to me His wonderful salvation. He has forgiven my sins, eradicated my sorrows, and brought me from terrible confinement into liberty. Behold the Lamb of God, Who takes away my sins! Behold the Lamb of God, Who takes away your sins as well! Come, therefore, and with tears of repentance and love let us kiss the wounds of this Lamb, Who took upon Himself the sins of the world. You, Infinite Goodness, Lord of heaven and earth, send ever upon us Your blessing, evoke in us sincere repentance and love unfeigned, have patience on the world that still perishes in sins, and through Your marvelous signs awaken it from its grave, sinful sleep. Amen.

On Great and Holy Friday Before the Holy Shroud

And I, if I am lifted up from the earth, will draw all peoples to Myself (John 12:32). That is, if I am lifted up on the cross, then through My sufferings on the cross I will redeem the whole world, and through the power of My cross I will draw unto Me many chosen ones. This is what our Lord Jesus Christ said not long before He suffered for us. Oh, Christ, our love! And once again I say, oh Christ, our love! To what end did Your love for us lead You! You were spat on, beaten, wounded, and died in unspeakable sufferings on the cross. Oh, Christ, our love! How strongly You loved us!

Your sufferings for the world were great, without measure, but so much infinitely greater were the fruits of Your suffering: *by His stripes we are healed* (Isa 53:5). You accepted sufferings to free us from the passions. You accepted the crown of thorns so that our hearts would no longer be tormented miserably, as with prickly and burning needles, by the thorns of sins. You accepted wounds, so that repentant sinners would take shelter in Your wounds from the arrows of heavenly wrath, You suffered on the cross to give it to us as a powerful weapon against our invisible enemies, who strongly fight against us. Finally, You accepted the brutal torments of the cross in order to save Your faithful servants from the most cruel, unceasing torments of hell. The goal of doing this was a single one, to draw us to You and unite us with You for eternity.

Therefore, beloved, our Head, Christ, suffers, so that His whole body, that is, us, will be free of pain. Our Head burns with the fire of the torments on the cross to deliver His members from sin and from eternal fire. Who can grasp with his mind, or feel with his heart, the full worth of this good deed? Only He knows fully how great was His sacrifice for us, because only He knew, and saw, how real are the eternal torments of sinners, and how cruel are the eternal torments, when He spoke of sinners: *these will go away into everlasting punishment* (Matt 25:46), which indisputably will come upon unrepentant sinners. *We can barely form a conjecture of the things upon the earth, and the things at hand we find with toil;* we very often do not understand the full misery of our present state, *but the things that are in heaven*, that is, what will come after death, *who hath searched out* (Wis 9:16)? Oh, our most precious Saviour! What shall we render unto You for Your infinitely great sacrifice for us? Faith and love. Hence, beloved, believe with your whole hearts, without the least shred of doubt, that the Only-Begotten, Incarnate Son of God suffered for you as well, namely, for you, in order to deliver you from eternal torments, which we should have suffered according to the justice of the Heavenly Father, and which we will suffer now if we will not have faith in His Son with our whole hearts, Who took upon Himself the sins of the world, and will not observe His commandments. Bring His suffering closer to your hearts, evaluate them as you can with your weak minds, and let each one of you burn with gratitude to God, without murmuring his own sorrows, illnesses, and sufferings, and let your hearts burn with the fire of love for Him Who out of love for you underwent the agonizing fire of physical and spiritual sufferings.

Let lack of love, hatred, and discord amongst yourselves flee from each and every one of you; because our mutual lack of love and hatred, like arrows, pierce the heart of the Lord, Who loved us unto the cross and death, and they exclude us from among His followers. Let no one bind his heart to the world and its pleasures, There is no place for us in this world. No, our place is in heaven: *I desire that they also whom You gave Me may be with Me where I am* (John 17:24), said the Saviour regarding His followers. *For our citizenship is in heaven* (Phil 3:20), says the Apostle. The world with its riches is not worthy of us; it is heaven that must be in our thoughts and our hearts. Let us be transported up there, with our thoughts and desires, more often.

Having suffered willingly for our sake, Lord Jesus Christ, Son of God, You said on the way to Your sufferings: *And I, if I am lifted up from the earth, will draw all peoples to Myself.* Through Your grace, draw us unto Yourself in the kingdom. Amen.

On Great and Holy Friday
Before the Holy Shroud

I see a man who was tortured, killed, wrapped in a shroud, and placed in a tomb. But, who is he? Who is this victim of malice and revenge? He is not simply a man, but a God-Man, the Son of the Living God, Jesus Christ. And for what reason was the innocent, sinless, just God-Man killed, He Who is full of infinite love? Who killed Him, and where was He killed? He was killed because He loved mankind as no one had ever loved, and those who needed to understand this love did not want to understand it. He was killed because He did much for them, gave them countless blessings, the like of which no one before Him had done, and yet these blessings were wrongly interpreted. He was killed because He performed many great and beneficial miracles, such miracles no one before had performed, and yet the people looked at these miracles with malice. He was killed because He called Himself, when it was necessary,

Who He really was, that is, the Son of God who came into the world to save sinners. He was killed because He denounced flagrant iniquities. He was killed because the whole world, all the people followed Him, who were witnesses of His blessings and recipients of His miracles, and who, however, soon forgot these blessings and miracles. These are the reasons for which the God-Man was killed. Who killed Him? The Jews, the same people who killed the prophets who denounced their iniquities and lawlessness before the coming of the Saviour; the Jews, the chosen people of God, who received from God countless blessings, astounding miracles, of which the Orthodox Church sings daily until now.

Moreover, here lies a great mystery, which especially now all of us ought to grasp. The tormenters and murderers of the Son of God were not only the Jews and pagan Romans; all of us are also very guilty of these torments and of this murder. Why? Because the Son of God, Jesus Christ, as Saviour of the world, was sacrificed for our sins; by suffering and dying, He received from the All-Just Heavenly Father upon His humanity the punishment for all our sins. The Jews did to the God-Man the same thing that perhaps all of us would have done through our passions had we been in their place. And to speak honestly, we now do similar things, albeit in a smaller scale and in a different manner, to our neighbors. Therefore, look closely upon this

Divine Sufferer, Who was dead for three days. This is the offering for our sins. This is the offering of God's infinite love for the world that lies in sin, and, consequently, His love toward me and toward you, beloved brother. The Son of God took upon Himself, instead of me and you, all of the horrors of eternal justice, of eternal punishment, that were due to me and to you; He drank the cup of the righteous wrath and fury of the Almighty God that should have been drunk by me and you. He took upon Himself all of the flaming arrows from God's quiver, prepared for sinners, that should have eternally struck and scorched me and you, ungrateful and depraved sinners.

So, fellow sinners! Fear adding sin to sin, transgression upon transgression. Looking upon this divine Sufferer, learn from now on and forever to hate and despise every sin, and to love truth and virtue. If we willingly and consciously add sin upon sin, we will crucify the Son of God within ourselves often and repeatedly; if we repent hypocritically and commune unworthily of the divine mysteries, if after confessing our sins and communing of the Holy Mysteries for purification and sanctification we live fearlessly on the whims of our corrupt hearts, then these same wounds on the hands, feet, and sides of our Saviour will be unto us not for salvation, but for condemnation, and then no one will save us from the torments of Gehenna for all eternity.

My brethren! Let us bring to the Lord, Who suffered and died for us, tears of sincere repentance and compunction, and let us live in constant repentance and good deeds. Amen.

HOMILY 37

On Great and Holy Friday

O, Life, how is it that You die? (Hymn on Great Saturday)

Let all of creation come: let us offer parting hymns to the Creator. Countless hosts of the heavenly powers! All of the rational inhabitants of the earth! Come, let us offer parting hymns to our common Creator, Who after such cruel sufferings now lies peacefully in the tomb! Let us approach Him and ask Him, "Why have You died, Who lives on high and Whom the heavens cannot contain, and now wondrously lies in a small tomb?" How is it that You, the immortal Creator of life, tasted death Yourself, and how were You placed dead in the tomb? How did this happen, that Your feeble, and yet vicious, creation, men, brought You to the grave? It is clear that You willingly allowed Your flesh to ascend on the cross, otherwise, who would have dared to touch You, the Almighty? Clearly a great mystery is at work here, one of which neither your evildoers nor the prince of darkness himself knew. And in fact, the people did not know what they did to Jesus Christ. It is clear that from Your extreme condescension toward people much good happened to them, because all that You do is only for the multiplication of good and blessings for creation. It must be that You suffered because of a great need, with a most wise and merciful purpose, for *in wisdom You have made them all* (Ps 104:24), and *the Lord is good to all* (Ps 145:9); is it possible that Your sufferings and death were not the works of Your infinite wisdom and goodness? Listen, brethren, the answer from the Lord Himself, Who suffered for us: *Unless a grain of wheat falls into the ground and dies, it remains alone: but if it dies, it produces much grain* (John 12:24).

Therefore, brethren, this is what the mystery of the death of Jesus Christ, God and Man, consists of. Just as the grain of wheat after falling on the ground, if it does not die, it remains alone, but if it dies, then it produces much grain, likewise did the Saviour die to bring the greatest benefit to people through His death, as it in fact happened. Christ, the Saviour, the Son of God, took upon Himself a great deed, to redeem, to justify us sinners before the Heavenly Father through His sufferings and death. This is *our justification* (Rom 4:25), says the Apostle, and, His death for us, with the sufferings that preceded it, is a deed of God's greatest wisdom and love for us, which cannot be worthily appreciated by any created mind. As this death is a deed of God's wisdom, it is also a great mystery. What a comforting truth! The death of the Saviour is a sacrifice of purification for the sins of the whole world. *He Himself is the propitiation*, says the Apostle John the Theologian, *for our sins, and not for ours only but also for the whole world* (1 John 2:2). He died, and His death on the cross destroyed our curse, which we deserved from the Heavenly Father because of our sins. He died, and the eternal death, which inevitably should have befallen us were it not for the Redeemer, now no longer has power over us. He is our truth among our falsehood, our salvation at the time of our despair, our sanctification among our impurities. He is the light in our darkness, life in our death. Are you afraid of the righteous judgment of God when you think of your iniquity? And is there *no health in* your *bones because of* your *sin* (Ps 38:4)? The sufferings and death of Jesus Christ justify you before the Heavenly Father. *It is God who justifies. Who is he who condemns? It is Christ who died, and furthermore is also risen, who is even at the right hand of God, who also makes intercession for us* (Rom 8:33-34).

Do you despair of not entering the kingdom of heaven, thinking you are unworthy of it? True, no one is worthy of it. But Christ, our Lord, is worthy; He acquired the kingdom for us through His priceless Blood. Our worthiness depends on His worthiness. Through His worthiness He made us, who are unworthy, worthy.

Through His grace, His Heavenly Father, Who is good and loves mankind through His ineffable mercy, grants people the kingdom of heaven. You may say, I am a great sinner. But Christ the Saviour *came into the world to save sinners* (1 Tim 1:15). Just do not sin intentionally and with malice in the future. You may say, how can I rejoice and be with the saints, who shone forth on earth with such virtues? But the saints were saved through Christ's grace. If to you it seems too much to be together with the saints, then pray to at least be together with the thief, crying: *Lord, remember me when You come into Your kingdom* (Luke 23:42), and try to live as a Christian should.

All of us, brethren, are sinners; however, if we believe in our Lord Jesus Christ, Who was crucified for us, and try to live according to His teachings, if we resist sin, or, even if we fall, we rise back up again, then the death of our Saviour, His wounds, will be our shield (Rom 3:25); we will flee the torments of hell and will be made worthy of the kingdom of heaven. If we magnanimously bear sorrows, illness, deprivation, and various misfortunes in our life and account them as being the due reward for our sins, remembering with faith and love the terrible sufferings the Lord endured for us, then we will be blessed: the crucified Saviour will save us. However, woe to them who are Christians only in name and trample on His saving teachings through their disregard for Him, or through their impertinent philosophizing about Him

(Rom 2:8), who live according to their hearts in falsehood, impurity, in forgetfulness of God: they must be terrified of their terrible situation, for *it is a fearful thing to fall into the hands of the living God* (Heb 10:31). *He will destroy those wicked men miserably* (Matt 21:41). The death of the Life-Giver does not save unrepentant sinners, but condemns them; but those sinners who sincerely repent of their falls into sin, and who have heartfelt faith in the Lord, hope in Him, and cleanse themselves from their sins, are saved by Him; through His sufferings on the cross the Saviour covers their sins committed due to human weakness. O Christ our God, Who was crucified, trampling down death by death, save us! Amen.

On Great and Holy Friday

My God, My God, why have You forsaken Me? (Matt 27:46)

Such was the cry of the Lamb of God, the Lord Jesus Christ, nailed on the cross for the sins of the world, and, consequently, for our sins, brothers and sisters. *My God, My God, why have You forsaken Me?* He cried according to His human nature, which had weaknesses, but not sin. But how could God the Father have abandoned His only begotten Son, Who had sent Him to the world to save it? The divinity was, and remains throughout the ages, inseparable from the human nature of Jesus Christ. This abandonment, beloved brethren, means that the human nature in Jesus Christ was left to experience all of the torments, all of the terrible sufferings on the cross, all of the horrible, deadly afflictions He experienced while still in the garden of Gethsemane before being arrested by the mob of villains led by Judas Iscariot. Already then He started to tremble and grieve, and told the disciples: *My soul is exceeding sorrowful, even to death. Stay here and watch with Me* (Matt 26:38).

Imagine then the bodily torments, the sorrow that was felt by the most just and all-loving sensitive soul of the God-Man, Who suffered the punishment for all the sins of men, for the sins of Adam and Eve and all of their descendants without exception, meaning, for your and our sins as well! And we, brethren, are greater sinners and guilty of countless punishments for our countless transgressions. Judge, I say, judge how sharp, bitter, and pungent the sufferings on the cross were, what sorrow the Lamb of God, Who took upon Himself the sins of the world, felt in His soul, how difficult it was for Him to be forsaken by God, that is, to have His human nature experience all of the bitter sufferings in His soul, all of the overwhelming, limitless, terrible affliction. After this you will understand in what condition was the soul of the God-Man nailed to the cross, when He cried out: *My God, My God, why have You forsaken Me?* Yes, His soul was together with His Most-Pure Body in terrible conditions, in unimaginable and indescribable suffering.

Perceive from this, man, whoever you may be, the bitterness, absurdity, dishonor, vileness, madness, ugliness, agony, and the deadliness of sin. Perceive how it is contrary to our nature, incompatible with our divine nature, created according to God's image; and how the

All-holy, All-perfect, and All-good Divinity despises it, and after this judge, all of you, how we should relate to sin that entices, defiles, and perverts our nature, corrupting it and plunging it into eternal disgrace, eternal sorrow, and eternal torment, if we do not despise it, that is, sin, with all our soul, if we do not repent of our transgressions, if we do not turn away completely from sin. Imagine, picture what would have happened to us if the Only Begotten Son of God had not suffered for our sins, if He had not satisfied God's justice, and if God had left us forever without His grace? A simple thought, just the idea of this chills the blood, and makes our soul tremble. If only I, and all sinners, always remembered, especially at the times when we are tempted by sin, how God forsakes unrepentant sinners, then all of us would flee from sin more than we would flee from snakes, from bloodthirsty beasts, from cruel enemies. Then there would be many more people among those who are saved, and the earth would not be struck by terrible disasters because of the sins of men: bad harvests, floods, devastating earthquakes, affecting thousands of human lives, epidemic diseases, damaged crops, destructive fires.

Then the earth would be God's paradise, abounding with truth and all of the natural gifts of God. Then there would be peace and security on the earth; there would not be terrible atrocities, among which we recently saw the worst of all, the brazen and malicious murder of the gentle, meek, and peace-loving Grand Duke [Sergei Alexandrovich] in broad daylight. Oh, how the world is now overflowing with transgressors and transgressions! How much longer will this sinful world survive, this earth, this gathering of every abomination, this habitation of sin, stained with the blood of pure and innocent victims? Has the time not come for the universal purification by fire? Yes, the time is certainly at hand. If the Apostles during their own time already spoke of its proximity, then we can even more readily speak of the proximity of the end of time.

Brothers and sisters! While we still have time, let us approach the Saviour of the world with ardent repentance, and with love and tears let us kiss His wounds, which He suffered for us. Let us love truth, let us love mercy, so that we may be shown mercy. Amen.

On St Thomas Sunday

Christ is risen! (1 Cor 15:20)

Beloved brethren, Bright Week has passed and carried with it our deeds to present them at the throne of the Heavenly Master and Judge, our deeds, brethren, are there now. I say this to put the fear of God on those who spent the feast of the Bright Resurrection of Christ in an unworthy and unchristian manner, and also to console those who spent it in temperance and spiritual joy.

How did many people greet and spend the feast of the Bright Resurrection? I have no desire to bring to mind the abominable deeds of men, but it is necessary to remember them and condemn them on behalf of God together with the people who performed them. The bright feast was greeted after the Easter services with dark deeds: intemperance and drunkenness, fights, swearing, and every kind of sin. You would think that we fasted before the feast only so we could even more eagerly engage in all sinful, carnal deeds, so we could give ourselves over to every transgression with even more shamelessness and impudence. Alas! Woe, woe to us!

All of those who greeted the feast with intemperance and drunkenness, adultery, swearing, and other carnal deeds such as these lost every benefit they received (if they even received any) from the fast, they lost the benefits received from repentance and the communion of the Holy Mysteries; they trampled on them with their feet like irrational animals, they lost the time favorable for salvation, given to us by the Lord's mercy, and they cannot have this time back. *Behold, now is the accepted time; behold, now is the day of salvation* (2 Cor 6:2) was proper to say to you during the holy fast, for then you had just entered the saving bath of repentance and approached the Mysteries of the Lord's Body and Blood, which purify the faithful. From now on your confession and communion are set aside until the next fast, and who knows whether or not the Lord will grant you once again confession and communion? Who knows whether or not you will die with these same sins with which you have defiled yourselves once again after the bath of repentance? How painful, how pitiful, my beloved brethren, that you so quickly showed yourselves to be traitors of Christ and went over to the side of the devil, in order to serve him, the original murderer, author and teacher of all sin! You, in the words of the Saviour, as well as I, a great sinner, *are of your father the devil, and the desires of your father you want to do* (John 8:44).

What is left for us to do, beloved brethren? To pray and to weep for our sins. To weep over the fact that many of us greeted the feast in an unchristian, and even inhuman, manner, but greeted it like loathsome idolaters and like wild beasts that were not fed for a long time, who for a long time were not fed their favorite food. We must weep over the fact that we trampled over the greatest, soul-saving Mysteries of Christ, confession and communion, and wasted them. We must weep over the fact that we have recklessly lost the time that was given us for salvation. Let us weep and pray to the Lord, so that He *will not be angry with us until the end, and will not destroy us with our iniquities* (excerpt from the Morning Prayers), but will turn us to the path of repentance and make us skilled observers of His commandments. Let us firmly decide from now on to never again give ourselves over to intemperance and drunkenness and all the sins that come from them, and let us ask the Lord with tears that He may strengthen us, through the grace of the Holy Spirit, in our intentions and good deeds.

Brethren! Let us all shed tears, for all of us have unworthily greeted the greatest feast of the Lord, and all of us have angered our Lord. Truly, this is not the way in which all of us should greet the feasts of the Lord. We should greet them with spiritual joy in the Lord, for being delivered from sins and having received eternal salvation through Christ, the Son of God. We should greet them with deeds of mercy, by abstaining from the passions, by attending God's temple in spirit and truth, and by simplicity in food and clothing.

And you, women and maidens, who are adorned with gold and precious fabrics! On behalf of the Lord I turn to you with a word! How many poor people could you have brought joy to in the bright day of Christ's Resurrection, and thus worthily greeted this great feast day, if out of generosity and Christian love you had converted but a few of your adornments into money and had given this money to the poor, of which we have so many in our city? How wise, in a Christian manner, you would have been if you possessed fewer precious garments and instead used the money left over from such purchases to give to those in need! What rich mercy you would receive on that day from Christ our Lord! Yes, then you would have greeted the feast of Christ's Resurrection in a truly Christian manner.

But now what? You are adorned like idols, but the members of Christ have nothing to wear. You are full, but the members of Christ are hungry. You are immersed in all possible manner of pleasure, while they are weeping. We live in rich and decorated houses, but they live in small and unclean houses, which often are no better than barns. We have no Christian love, we also have no true feast day of Christ's Resurrection. He truly celebrates the resurrection who rises from lifeless deeds to the deeds of virtue, to faith and Christian love, who tramples on intemperance, luxury, and all the passions. Brethren! Let us celebrate the feasts of the Lord as Christians, and not as pagans! Amen.

SUBJECT INDEX

SCRIPTURE INDEX